Speaker

DRIVING RESULTS

DRIVING RESULTS

SIX LESSONS LEARNED
FROM TRANSFORMING AN ICONIC COMPANY

GARY A. GARFIELD

WILEY

Published by John Wiley & Sons, Inc., Hoboken, New Jersey.
Published simultaneously in Canada.

For general information on our other products and services or for technical support, please contact our Customer Care Department within the United States at (800) 762-2974, outside the United States at (317) 572-3993 or fax (317) 572-4002.

Wiley publishes in a variety of print and electronic formats and by print-on-demand. Some material included with standard print versions of this book may not be included in e-books or in print-on-demand. If this book refers to media such as a CD or DVD that is not included in the version you purchased, you may download this material at http://booksupport.wiley.com. For more information about Wiley products, visit www.wiley.com.

Library of Congress Cataloging-in-Publication Data

Names: Garfield, Gary A., author.
Title: Driving results : six lessons learned from transforming an iconic
    company / Gary A. Garfield.
Description: Hoboken, New Jersey : Wiley, [2022] | Includes index.
Identifiers: LCCN 2022015061 (print) | LCCN 2022015062 (ebook) | ISBN
    9781119822479 (cloth) | ISBN 9781119822493 (adobe pdf) | ISBN
    9781119822486 (epub)
Subjects: LCSH: Bridgestone Americas, Inc. | Corporate
    turnarounds–Management.
Classification: LCC HD58.8 .G3695 2022 (print) | LCC HD58.8 (ebook) | DDC
    658.4/06–dc23/eng/20220401
LC record available at https://lccn.loc.gov/2022015061
LC ebook record available at https://lccn.loc.gov/2022015062

Cover Design: Wiley
Cover Image: © zhaojiankang/Getty Images

SKY10034444_051922

*To my family. From my great-grandmother, who immigrated
to the United States from Kyiv (then Kiev) with two young
boys (ultimately my grandfather and uncle) in the early
twentieth century so her family and future generations could
have a better life; to my parents and grandparents, who so
often guided me; to my wife, who supported my efforts; and
to my kids and grandchildren, who have always inspired me
to be my best.*

Contents

Introduction

SEARS IS AN extraordinary study in corporate change. It grew its fortunes as a mail-order retailer. Its first mail order catalog was in 1883, selling watches and jewelry. By 1896, the iconic Sears catalog included bicycles, clothes, groceries, pianos, medical supplies, cars, and even kits to build houses. The mail-order retailer filled a great need as our country spread out to small, rural towns and family farms with few nearby retail outlets.

Then, as Americans increasingly moved to cities and suburbs and had greater access to shopping centers and malls in the latter half of the twentieth century, Sears adapted. It reduced its reliance on mail order and was instead an anchor store for malls all over the country. It became the largest retailer in the world, and it had the extraordinary deftness to alter its business model from mail order to brick and mortar. In 1993, it ceased producing its famed catalog altogether.

But then the company became stale. Its name and brands lost their luster. Business drastically declined as Walmart superstores and other big box stores grew, along with other specialty retailers such as Best Buy and Home Depot. Its management team had lost the agility or foresight that had been demonstrated in the not-too-distant past.

Then, ironically, came Amazon, in effect today's dominant mail order retailer. Sears attempted to recreate its former extraordinary mail-order (that is, online) business, but the effort failed. The Amazon juggernaut further hurt shopping malls, and Sears filed for bankruptcy protection in 2018.

The point, however, is much bigger than Sears alone. The bottom line is everything changes, all the time, and absolutely nothing can be done to prevent it. "Change or die." "Change is not mandatory; survival is optional." "When you're finished changing, you're finished."

Those businesses that have the vision and drive to change will thrive as Sears did when it initially transformed from mail-order to brick and mortar. Those that can't keep changing will, ultimately, join the corporate obituary pages like Sears.

Of course, Sears is not unique in failing to successfully change. But in the merciless, survival of the fittest world of a free-market economy, at some point or another most companies will fail if they don't adapt, if they don't change. All companies large or small need to continuously adjust to the changing environment in which they exist. Those that do survive and perhaps excel, those that do not, perish.

Blockbuster succumbed to Netflix; showing a fatal lack of vision, Blockbuster declined an offer to purchase Netflix for $50 million early on in Netflix's growth. Today, Netflix's market cap exceeds $200 billion and Blockbuster is nowhere to be found.

Polaroid gave way to the iPhone camera and digital film. Toys "R" Us also fell to Amazon. Perhaps nothing could have been done to prevent their ultimate demise given the extraordinary innovations of the iPhone and online shopping. But perhaps they would still be around today if they had the vision, the leadership, and executed the other essential elements of successfully driving change.

Camera stores and bookstores used to be commonplace, as did full-service gas stations. Those companies and businesses fell to changing technology.

Consumer preferences also necessitate change. Zenith TVs, Pontiac cars – gone; yet both televisions and cars are still very much in vogue. Budweiser is under pressure from craft beers, Diet Pepsi from healthier alternatives. Compaq didn't fail because computers became obsolete, nor did Yahoo falter because search engines became a thing of the past.

What will happen to automobile service stations as the car industry moves away from combustion engines to electric vehicles? There certainly will not be any oil to change, tune-ups to perform, or engines to rebuild. The coal industry is almost certainly going to become a relic of the past. Longer term, the same is likely true of other fossil fuel industries.

Yet, as constant as change is, and as imperative as it is, making change happen seems to be extraordinarily difficult. We are, as the saying goes, creatures of habit. We know this to be true. Trying to change an old habit, like nail-biting or cracking joints, is enormously hard. Similarly, trying to start a new habit is equally challenging. Most New Year's resolutions to exercise regularly or read a certain number of books a year, or whatever it may be, so often fall by the wayside. Thus, one of my friends proudly said they never failed to execute upon any of their resolutions because they didn't bother to make any.

As hard as change is for an individual, it is at least as hard for an organization, or even just a team of people such as a department or division of an organization. The momentum, the habits, the actions, the attitudes, and the beliefs of many people all must change and become aligned, not just one person. Accordingly, some have estimated that about 70 percent of all corporate change efforts fail.[1] Others take issue with that statistic, saying the data isn't clear and the failure rate isn't that abysmal. None dispute, however, that change is hard and fails to achieve its desired results a very significant percent of the time.

---

[1] See Boris Ewenstein, Wesley Smith, and Ashvin Sologar, "Changing Change Management," McKinsey, July 1, 2015.

This book was written against these two premises – one, the necessity for businesses to change and, two, the difficulty in making change happen. Specifically, this book is intended to address the glaring need to help leaders drive the changes they think are required for their team, department, division, company, or organization to not only survive, but thrive.

Of course, it is ultimately the responsibility of the leader to decide upon the correct path, and I cannot do that for them. Such a decision requires a deep analysis of the business issues and the likely state of the market down the road. Having made that critical decision, a leader is then faced with the challenging task of making the decision become a reality. That is where this book can be of value.

This book is written from real-world experiences and lessons learned in advising and working with a number of different executives and organizations, including the hands-on experience and success at driving change at Bridgestone Americas.

Bridgestone Americas is an excellent example of how companies can adapt, change, and withstand the test of time. In the United States, the story begins with Firestone. Firestone is an iconic brand, going back to its founding by Harvey Firestone. In 1900, Firestone started producing pneumatic tires, and those tires could be found on most Ford automobiles, as well as many other cars. The company grew to a great conglomerate, a massive Firestone empire. Over time, however, like many mature organizations, the once great company struggled for several reasons in the 1960s and 1970s, but certainly not because tires became less relevant. Rather, with the rise of automobile ownership and shipping by truck, tires were more relevant to the US economy than ever.

In 1988, Firestone corporation was acquired by a Japanese company, Bridgestone Corporation. Firestone was, ultimately, renamed Bridgestone Americas, and was the largest subsidiary of what is today one of the largest tire and rubber companies in the world, Bridgestone Corporation. Bridgestone Americas (that is, the former Firestone Tire and Rubber company along with most Bridgestone operations in the Western Hemisphere) consisted of some 55,000 employees operating on five continents. Tire manufacturing, marketing, and sales was the core of its business, but it also had several other businesses.

Like all companies, shareholders continually demanded stronger results, but they were hard to come by in the ultra-competitive tire industry.

In 2010, I was appointed the CEO and a colleague was appointed to the new position of chief operating officer of Bridgestone Americas. These appointments were certainly a surprise to the organization. Prior to becoming the CEO, I was vice president, general counsel, and chief compliance officer of Bridgestone Americas. I was a lawyer. The COO had been head of the company's Latin American operations.

From day one, we embarked on driving a series of changes throughout the organization. Everything was in play: culture, people, organizational structure, business models, strategy, and so on.

The changes worked. It wasn't always perfect or even pretty, but they worked. The organization had record-breaking success. We achieved record profits every year of my tenure. Indeed, operating profits grew fivefold from 2010 to 2016, something that no one had thought possible. At the same time cash flow dramatically improved as well, allowing the organization to both reduce unwanted debt and invest in its future. This was all achieved organically. Because of these extraordinary results, several of the changes we made were emulated throughout the global Bridgestone organization.

Through the massive change journey of Bridgestone Americas as well as my work with other organizations and executives, it became clear that there are six essential requirements to successfully driving change. These six requisites are the lessons learned from my various experiences, and each must be applied with equal force to drive change in a team of people, departments, divisions, or entire organizations. With these six lessons, a change effort is highly likely to succeed. That is, the changes that the leader envisions will come to fruition. Hopefully, of course, the leader's vision, that is the type and nature of the changes, are the correct ones for the business and market dynamics. One thing is certain, however, without any one of these requisites of change, the change effort will almost certainly fall short of the mark if not fail entirely.

Part I of this book discusses first the results that were achieved due to the significant, indeed, massive changes made at Bridgestone Americas. Most readers are unaware of this success story, and it puts into context a primary motivation and story behind this book. Part I then provides a brief background on Bridgestone Americas to provide context for the reader. I discuss some of the history of the magnificent Bridgestone and Firestone empires which led to the merging of the two companies, and some of the post-merger challenges the organization faced. Part I then discusses in general terms the typical evolution of most companies. While the life cycle of organizations is well-documented,[2] it also helps in understanding the importance of change for many organizations. Part I then closes by discussing some of the key warning signs – both external and internal to the organization – that it is time for management to consider significant changes to the organization.

Part II explains each of the six requirements or lessons learned to implement effective change: Leadership, Vision, Culture, People, Alignment, and Focused Execution. Others might label these requirements differently or they may break them down in a different way than I do, but substantively, I firmly believe that each of these keys are essential for a meaningful and successful transformation process. In the context of those chapters, the

---

[2] Corporate Finance Institute, "Business Life Cycle: The 5 Stages of a Business's Life," https://corporatefinanceinstitute.com/resources/knowledge/finance/business-life-cycle/.

book explains many of the specific changes implemented during Bridgestone Americas' highly successful journey. I use these examples to help the reader understand, in depth, the importance of each key requirement of successful transformation.

The book provides many examples to help the reader better understand the specific point at issue. While some of these examples were loosely derived from observations and anecdotes, both before and after Bridgestone Americas, some of these examples are fictional. Where the examples were derived from stories I had seen or heard in my work, whether with Bridgestone Americas or advising other companies or executives, the people and events have been changed to protect everyone and any similarities to actual persons or events are entirely coincidental.

This book benefits you, the reader, in two distinct ways. First, readers will get several ideas for specific changes that may benefit them in their respective situation. For example, you will learn about cultural change levers and how leaders can use them to drive cultural changes among a team of people. Or, ideas on how to align cultural changes with performance reviews or how we sold the notion of massive changes to an organization that did not know change of any form was needed.

Second, and arguably far more important, you will learn and understand the six requirements or lessons of successfully driving those changes you want to make, and how to deploy the elements of change in your particular situation. Of course, change requires leadership. But what does that really mean and why does organizational change fail to happen despite a leader who wants change? What is corporate culture, why does it matter, and how does one actually go about altering the deeply ingrained behaviors and focus of people throughout a team, department, or organization? Many leaders struggle with people decisions as they are driving change; hopefully, my experiences and insight will help the leader struggle less and act more.

Importantly, these six lessons of successfully transforming a company can be used not only by CEOs, but also by a leader in just about every context and position. Whether it be a team, department, function or project leader, civic team, or other organization, these keys to change are applicable. In other words, the principles of successful transformation apply to just about all levels and most situations involving significant change.

It is my firm belief that, armed with a deep understanding of the six lessons to successfully driving change, a leader's change efforts will succeed rather than, as all too often happens, fail. Rather than being one of the roughly 70 percent of change efforts that don't work or falls short, the leader's change efforts will achieve or exceed the results that they envision just as our change efforts produced results beyond our expectations at Bridgestone Americas.

PART I

The Change Imperative

1

Success Through Change

WHO AM I to write this book on change? What are my qualifications? What have I accomplished that gives me any credibility on the subject? These are legitimate questions, and I will do my best to address them up front.

The answer is this: Bridgestone Americas is the largest subsidiary of one of the largest tire and rubber companies in the world, Bridgestone Corporation, headquartered in Tokyo, Japan. Bridgestone Americas is responsible for the tire operations in North, South, and Central America, and it also has several businesses apart from tires, some of which are global in scope.[1] Bridgestone Americas employed some 55,000 people operating on five continents.

When I was vice president and general counsel of Bridgestone Americas in 2009, its annual revenues were roughly $10 billion and its operating profits were roughly $300 million. As is the case with just about every company, the shareholders wanted stronger results.

---

[1] Since the time of my retirement in 2016, Bridgestone Americas sold one of its larger non-tire businesses, Firestone Building Products.

In 2010, my first year as CEO at Bridgestone Americas, the company achieved record operating profits with a roughly 20 percent improvement over the year before, and a roughly threefold improvement over the historical average for the prior six years. The following year – 2011 – was more successful still. Operating profits grew by roughly 75 percent. No one in the organization imagined Bridgestone Americas would make over $700 million in a single year, but it did. Bridgestone Americas was significantly outperforming other parts of the Bridgestone organization around the globe.

With the record achievements of 2011 in the books, the possibility of reaching $1 billion in operating profits on an annual basis – something that was previously unfathomable – became a possibility. No one dared dream that we would achieve such a milestone in 2012, a roughly 40 percent profit improvement over 2011.

We created a special incentive program (alignment of rewards to outcomes) to try to achieve that remarkable milestone in one year's time. The team worked extremely hard to realize that goal. All our efforts worked. We surpassed $1 billion in profit, and we paid everyone very handsomely for their efforts. Ultimately, by the end of 2015, Bridgestone Americas' profits had grown over fivefold from where they had started when I took over the helm.

From 2010 to 2016, when I retired, Bridgestone Americas operating profit growth outperformed the average for the S&P 500 companies over that period. Each year was a record and by a significant amount. Our revenues went from about $10 billion to over $15 billion. Importantly, cash flow improved by hundreds of millions of dollars. With the influx of cash, much of our unwanted debt melted away. We invested large amounts of money in our people, brands, manufacturing capabilities, technology, and the future of the company.

One of our key performance goals was to improve our Return on Assets (ROA) from roughly 1 percent to 5 percent. By focusing on the fundamentals of being a profitable company, fulfilling our brand promise, and being a premier place to work, our ROA improved to over 9 percent by 2016.

At the beginning of the change effort in 2010, Bridgestone Americas represented about 38 percent of the global Bridgestone revenue and roughly 10 percent of the worldwide profits. When I retired in 2016, Bridgestone Americas represented 50 percent of both the revenue and profits of the global Bridgestone organization. Bridgestone Americas not only carried its weight; it was by far the largest part of the global Bridgestone organization. With Bridgestone Americas' success, the global Bridgestone organization became the largest tire and rubber company in the world.

All of this was achieved organically – that is, without the quick improvements in revenues and profits that a large acquisition can provide. Within the Bridgestone family of companies, the Americas became the model that other parts of the worldwide Bridgestone organization sought to emulate. Our governance structure, strategic goals, culture, business strategies, marketing, and so on were studied and copied throughout the Bridgestone world.

The results, while very important, are not the whole story. There was much, much more. Teammates were more engaged, the energy was vibrant, and it showed in the work effort. We saw this firsthand, every day.

As a team we restored the iconic Firestone brand and helped rebuild a historic company. In the process, the team's tremendous efforts positively, and hopefully permanently, impacted thousands of employees and their families.

This success happened because of the many changes we made. We dared to take a different path than we had been taking. That is the power of successfully implementing change. And that is why this book has been written.

2

What Is Bridgestone Americas?

BRIDGESTONE IS A large, global company but it is not as well-known as, say, Coca-Cola, Disney, Apple, or Amazon. So, what is this company? What is Bridgestone Americas? It is hard to appreciate both the scope of the changes that we made and the reasons for many of the changes without a basic understanding of these questions.

Bridgestone Acquires Firestone

Bridgestone Americas' roots go back to the Firestone Tire and Rubber Company, founded by the remarkable Harvey Firestone in 1900. His company was best known for tires, but his business expanded over the years into an international conglomerate including, by way of example, department stores, automotive service centers, auto parts, beer kegs, gas tanks for fighter planes, and even radio and TV shows. In fact, the Voice of Firestone, which aired first on NBC and then ABC, ran for about fourteen years. The company was a global empire.

Mr. Firestone's success hinged on a few key business approaches. Build a great product, first and foremost. In fact, he believed a company had a duty to make such a good product that it wouldn't need to hire "cracker jack" salespeople.[1] Second, provide great customer service. For Mr. Firestone this included developing profound friendships with his customers. Firestone was the primary tire supplier to the Ford Motor Company, and Harvey became best of friends with Henry Ford. They, along with Thomas Edison, went "camping" together with their entourage of assistants. At least two sitting presidents of the United States joined the three "vagabonds," as they came to be known, on these famous camping trips across the American countryside. Their deep friendship extended to their families. The relationship between the Fords and the Firestones was real. Harvey's granddaughter married Henry's grandson.

The third business approach was to treat employees as family. Harvey built housing, parks, and schools near the tire factory in Akron so his workers would have everything they needed nearby. He created co-op loan services so his employees could buy their houses. He made it easier for his workers to have a comfortable life. He also insisted that stock in the company be part of every employee's compensation. They had to have a stake in the company's success, he argued. Every employee – not just the executives – was a member of the legendary Firestone Country Club. It was his company, and the employees were his family. To be sure, all of this helped his business, and it helped people too.

Some years after his passing in 1938, the vast company started to struggle. It had, in effect, become mature in its organizational life cycle. Global tire competition increased significantly, putting pressure on Firestone's sales and profits. The company also suffered from a series of crises. One disaster led to another, including

---

[1] Harvey S. Firestone, *Men and Rubber* (Garden City, NY: Doubleday, 1926).

various legal scandals, such as the 1949 "Great American Streetcar Scandal"[2] and later the vice-chairman embezzling from the company. But the single largest problem happened forty years after his death: the Firestone 500 radial tire recall in 1978.

Like all other American tire companies, Firestone historically had produced bias tires. The French tire company, Michelin, invented the radial tire, which provided superior performance and ultimately made bias tires largely obsolete.

The Firestone 500 was the company's first radial tire. About 23 million Firestone 500 radial tires were produced between 1971 and 1978, and they were extremely popular. But reports of Firestone 500 tire failures grew as time passed. Ultimately, in 1978, the company recalled about 14 million tires. It was one of the largest tire recalls in history.[3]

The recall cost the company hundreds of millions of dollars. Worse was the damage to its reputation, and therefore, sales revenue. By the end of the 1970s, the company was hemorrhaging money.

In 1980, John Nevin from Zenith was hired as CEO to save the iconic tire manufacturer. He was brought in to stop the financial losses and reduce the company's debt. He sold or closed several plants. He sold numerous other assets, including the Firestone Country Club, and he either sold or shut down unprofitable businesses.

---

[2] The scandal involved a conspiracy among several companies, including Firestone, to control city transit and eliminate electric street cars in favor of gasoline powered transportation.

[3] In fact, the data demonstrates that the adjustment rate (that is a measure of the frequency of tire failures) was no more for Firestone 500 tires than most other tire manufactures. Because Firestone produced such a huge quantity of tires under the Firestone 500 name, however, the number of failures became far more noticeable than other tire brands that had much smaller productions.

To his credit, Nevin's massive cuts and strong hand worked. He turned around the company and the price of the company's stock rose significantly. But the answer going forward was clear. As the tire industry was going through a rash of mergers in the 1980s, Firestone shareholders would be well-served if it was acquired by a company with stronger financial resources.

* * *

Across the Pacific Ocean, Bridgestone Corporation, Japan's largest tire company, was both strong and growing. Founded in 1933 by Shojiro Ishibashi, another remarkable entrepreneur, he adopted the Bridgestone name for his company. Ishibashi translated into English is "stonebridge." The story goes that Mr. Ishibashi inverted the translation to Bridgestone out of respect for Harvey Firestone, who he had never met, but admired from afar.

Probably because of the Japanese culture of incredible attention to detail, over time Bridgestone developed strong manufacturing capabilities, like many other Japanese companies.

Like Firestone, Bridgestone also grew into a large conglomerate, making everything from tires to golf balls to massive shock absorbers that go underneath buildings to insulate them from the shock of Japan's frequent earthquakes. And, like Firestone in the United States, Shojiro Ishibashi and the Bridgestone name became iconic in Japan. With its large market share, reputation for excellence, and high brand awareness in Japan and much of Asia, its future was bright.

Ultimately, Bridgestone sought to expand to the United States, then the largest tire market in the world. While Bridgestone made inroads into the US market, it was tough due to fierce competition. To assist its US business, in 1981 it purchased an aging Firestone tire plant outside Nashville, Tennessee, which John Nevin had put up for sale.

In 1988, following a series of consolidations in the global tire industry, Pirelli, then the largest Italian tire company, made a play for Firestone. It bid around $50 per share for the company, a considerable amount given that the stock had been selling for about $30 not long before the offer, and just a few years before that it was down in the teens. In Tokyo, Bridgestone decided that its last and best chance to become a true global tire company was to purchase the struggling Firestone. The bidding was on, and Bridgestone was not about to lose. After a few back and forth offers, Bridgestone decided to put an end to the bidding war by offering $80 per share. Pirelli bowed out at the rich price and Nevin was a hero for Firestone shareholders.

An iconic American company became Japanese-owned with the memories of WWII still relatively fresh in the US psyche, and Bridgestone more than doubled in size overnight. Bridgestone Americas, as it was ultimately named, was by far the largest part of the global Bridgestone organization and responsible for the organization's tire business (manufacturing, sales, marketing, etc.) throughout the Western Hemisphere as well as several other national and international businesses that had been part of Firestone.

Bridgestone paid a premium for Firestone with the hopes of strengthening the company and expanding its geography. But, like most large acquisitions, the process of integrating Firestone into Bridgestone did not come easily.

The Challenges of Integrating Firestone into Bridgestone

It is one thing to acquire a company. It is a wholly different thing to integrate the acquired company, people, processes, and culture into one organization. The integration process takes enormous focus, effort, and time. Failure to effectively integrate the two organizations into one coherent company will likely mean that the promised results of the acquisition fail to come to fruition. In some cases, it can even prove fatal for the acquiring company. In other words, the stakes in successfully integrating the two companies are often huge.

The integration of Firestone into Bridgestone faced several unique challenges. First, Bridgestone's home office was in Tokyo while Firestone's was in Akron, Ohio, half a world away. Zoom conference calls and cell phones didn't exist in the late 1980s and early 1990s. Email was still in its infancy. Communication was a challenge to be sure. The shear geographic distance, some 6,500 miles, between the senior executive teams meant the two senior teams were on radically different time zones, further complicating communication.

Then, of course, were the language barriers. Few, if any, Firestone executives spoke Japanese. Several, but not all, of the Japanese executives spoke some level of English, but the level of proficiency varied significantly. It was easy to lose a lot in translation, if you will.

A third challenge were the cultural differences between Japan and America. Neither is better than the other. But they are unquestionably different from one another. Indeed, the cultural differences between the two countries is arguably larger than the geographic distance between them. These differences were demonstrated repeatedly.

Of the many examples, two drive the point home.

Shortly after I arrived in Tokyo for the first time, I was excited to go exploring. I asked a woman at the front desk if she had an English map of the city. She was, like most Japanese, dressed to perfection and polite to a "T." She ran – yes, literally ran in her high heels and dress – to the far end of the roughly 30-foot-long front desk to grab a city map, and literally ran back. When I say ran, I mean it. She then ever so politely placed the map in the palm of her hands and graciously presented it to me as if it were a priceless artifact. She then followed up with an offer to help me with directions, all the while as gracious and serving as anyone. I had similar experiences when shopping in department stores or the like. Salespeople would literally run to find someone to wait on me who could speak English. Extraordinary customer service!

Of course, outstanding customer service can be found in the United States. But both the level of service and the consistency across the board in Japan is in stark contrast to anything I have experienced elsewhere in the world.

Another striking example occurred when I would leave Japan to the United States. Every time, as the plane pulled away from the gate at Narita Airport, the four or so workers who serviced that plane on the ground literally lined up on the tarmac and waved goodbye as the plane departed. It is safe to say no such thing occurs at US airports.

The cultural differences between the United States and Japan manifested themselves in some of the many differences between Firestone and Bridgestone. In Japan, factory workers wore uniforms and proudly displayed the Bridgestone name. The factory floors were spotless. Several factory employees would do team yoga or exercises together before their shift. To be sure, the plants were not perfect. Management and laborers had their differences. But it was, in all, extraordinary how well the Japanese plants functioned. Indeed, in 1968, Bridgestone received the prestigious Deming Award for excellence in quality management.

In contrast to Japan, in the 1990s the relationship between management and the line workers at manufacturing plants throughout the United States was generally not amicable. Rather than wearing a company uniform as did the workers in Japan, in the United States factory line workers would generally wear jeans and t-shirts. Rather than proudly displaying the company's name or logo on their shirts, they might display their union's name or logo. In fact, some wore their animosity toward their employer on their sleeve with some derogatory image or statement about the company. Team exercises would take the form of calling in sick to go deer hunting when the season opened. Absenteeism, a significant problem at many of the plants, spiked when hunting season opened.

For each of these and other reasons, integrating the Bridgestone and Firestone operations into one, efficient and effective company took time and persistence. Fortunately for all concerned, part of the Japanese culture is to be long-term oriented and persistent.

In 1991 Japan sent one of its top executives, Yoichiro Kaizaki, to help improve the operations, and with his strong operational skills and instincts, he did. He was rewarded with the global CEO position in 1993 and returned to Japan.

One of Kaizaki-san's lieutenant's, Masatoshi Ono, assumed his responsibilities only to be greeted with a massive labor strike in 1994.

Labor strikes were not that uncommon in the United States during that timeframe. The United Auto Workers' massive strikes against General Motors in 1996 and another in 1988 are testimony to the nature of labor relations at the time in the US auto industry. Few large manufacturers were immune from labor issues.

The Clinton Administration pushed hard to get the company to back down from its demands from the union, but Mr. Ono's resolve did not waiver. He was determined to get the company's cost structure under control. The strike drained the financial resources of the United Rubber Workers such that the union had to merge with the United Steel Workers to ensure continued solvency.

Finally, after roughly 10 months into the strike the two sides were able to reach a new contract.

Financially, the company's profits improved, in part because of the lower factory wages. What's more, we started to win back some of the business we had lost because of the strike. Within the company we were optimistic about our future. We won back some control of our cost structure and plant operations from the union. The company's financials continued to improve through the remainder of the decade, and the future, we thought, was ours. And for a while, it was.

The Firestone Tire Recall and the Clash with Ford

In the early 1990s, Ford started producing the Explorer. Over time, it became a huge success. As one of the first SUVs in the United States, it was marketed to "soccer moms," and wisely so. They loved it. Sizable, convenient, and the driver sat up high. The Explorer became one of Ford's best-selling vehicles.

Firestone had been Ford's largest tire supplier since early in their respective histories. Henry Ford and Harvey Firestone had a legendary friendship. The relationship between the two companies continued after Bridgestone acquired Firestone. So, not surprisingly, like many Ford cars, the Explorer was equipped with Firestone tires. For every Explorer that Ford sold, Bridgestone sold five tires (four tires plus a spare), and then it sold many more replacement tires to the "soccer moms" who owned the Explorer. This helped fill up Bridgestone's factories, reducing the company's per tire costs. Ford's success became Bridgestone's success, and this was certainly a part of the company's improved financial performance in the latter half of the 1990s.

While car manufacturers outsource tires to companies like Bridgestone, they still control the type of tire it specs for their vehicles, including the recommended air pressure for the tires. For whatever reason, Ford set the manufacturer recommended air pressure level for the Explorer tires at the lowest level permitted by industry standards for the weight (that is, a fully loaded Explorer) the tires were carrying. That is fine if the tires maintain their air pressure as the weight of the loaded vehicle was within the design parameter of the tire. But tires slowly lose air pressure over time and if they lose too much, the heat builds up in the tire and they can no longer safely carry the weight of the vehicle. At that time, very few vehicles had warning lights if tires were underinflated – otherwise known as a Tire Pressure Monitoring System (TPMS). Indeed, it was the subsequent Ford–Firestone crisis that prompted Congress to pass a law requiring new cars produced after September 2007 to have that technology.

However, in early 2000, a Houston TV station reported that several Firestone ATX tires on Ford Explorers lost their treads at highway speeds, causing the car to flip into a roll and resulting in death or other catastrophic injuries. The report had discovered about 30 such instances across the southern half of the country.

It was no coincidence that these events took place almost exclusively in the South and in the summer. Heat is the enemy of a tire. Because tires are layers of components that are in effect laminated and then "cured" together, extreme heat (as well as other factors) can cause parts of a tire to, in effect, delaminate. That is never a good thing as a car speeds down the highway at 70 plus miles per hour. Many of these incidents involved tires that were substantially low on air pressure, which causes more heat to build up in the tire, which puts the integrity of the tire at risk.

Until the 1970s, all gas stations were full service. In fact, they were often called "service stations" not "gas stations." A driver would pull next to a gas pump and the attendant would come out and say, "Fill 'er up?" Typically, the answer was yes and then the attendant would ask, "Check your oil and tires?" Again, the answer would typically be yes. And so, not only did the car get gasoline, but the air pressure in its tires was also checked on a regular basis.

This is no small matter. A tire substantially low on air pressure is, in the fullness of time, destined to fail. It is the air pressure in the tire that keeps the tire running at a temperature within its design parameters as it spins down a scorching highway in the summer heat. But full-service stations largely became a thing of the past during the gas shortages in the 1970s, and they were largely replaced by self-service gas stations. The cost went down for the driver as "service stations" minimized labor costs, but the risks went up as relatively few people checked their tire pressure regularly, if at all.

In any event, the Houston TV news report was ultimately picked up by other television stations and then by the national networks. This, in turn, prompted the National Highway Traffic and Safety Administration (NHTSA) to open an investigation into our tires on the Explorer. This was headline material, further putting the company in a bad light.

News reports increased and consumer concern toward Firestone tires grew through the summer. Finally, following extensive discussions and an analysis with Ford, on August 9, 2000, we announced a recall of about 6.5 million Firestone tires that were manufactured over the previous nine years.

Angry and fearful customers demanded that their tires be replaced immediately. Unfortunately, it would take many months to produce enough of the size and type of tire on the Explorer to replace the millions of recalled tires still on the road. So, Bridgestone took the extraordinary and extremely costly step of replacing the tires with those produced by our competitors. Few, if any companies, have done such a thing.

Over the following months, our disaster was often the lead story on the national news. At one count, there were well over 3,000 news reports on the Ford-Firestone crisis. We were the butt of jokes in cartoons and the late-night TV shows. David Letterman, host of the *Late Show*, jokingly put the head of public relations for the company as one of his top 10 worst jobs in America. The negative publicity was relentless, and with it both our valuable reputation and sales were shrinking.

At the same time, we were inundated with class action lawsuits filed across the country. In all, more than 100 class action lawsuits were filed against the company in the ensuing months. But the legal party, if you will, was just beginning. Hundreds and ultimately thousands of personal injury lawsuits were filed against the company as well. To further exacerbate the situation, Congress announced hearings into the Ford-Firestone recall.

From a staffing standpoint, this was overwhelming. We simply did not have enough people to deal with the flood of issues we faced. From an experience standpoint, we were out of our depth. Few management teams in the world had ever experienced anything like this frenzied crisis, and that was certainly true of us. We were thrown into a tizzy.

Then came the federal securities fraud class action lawsuits as well as a formal investigation by nearly all of the state attorneys general for potential violations of states' laws. These actions were ultimately followed by a federal criminal investigation by the United States Attorney's office in Southern Illinois.

Overnight, Bridgestone's profits turned to losses as sales of Firestone tires almost ground to a halt. At the same time, our costs soared as we were paying for the terribly expensive recall, and we were still making Firestone tires that the consuming public was now afraid to purchase. On top of it all were the smothering public relations and litigation-related costs. The "talking heads" predicted the end of the Firestone brand if not the end of the entire Bridgestone organization. The situation could hardly have been more dire.

In the first round of Congressional hearings Ford testified that Firestone made world-class tires. Ford sang a different song in the second round of Congressional hearings just a few weeks later. In his opening remarks, Jacques Nasser, Ford's CEO, went on the attack, and Bridgestone was in his line of fire. He singularly blamed us for the recall, claiming that Ford had been deceived by us and the whole problem was our tires.

With that, like sharks, the members of Congress and the media smelled blood in the water and went in for the kill. Bridgestone was ultimately blamed for the deaths of hundreds of people, our reputation was destroyed, and it truly was questionable whether the company would survive.

Not too long thereafter, Japan made a management change, a change that almost certainly saved the company. Mr. Ono, the CEO who had replaced Kaizaki-san in the mid-1990s, returned to Japan and retired. In his place, Japan named John Lampe, an extremely smart yet humble executive of great integrity, as the new CEO for the Americas. John had worked his entire career for the company and was admired and loved both by employees and independent tire dealers. In a book written about the recall by an investigative reporter, a chapter focusing on Lampe was called "Moses."[4] From the company's perspective, the author did not overstate the case.

As the crisis continued, our relationship with our largest single customer, the Ford Motor Company, continued to sour. Ford could not resist every opportunity to attack Bridgestone, blaming its tires for the crisis in an attempt to distance itself from the disaster. Indeed, during the course of litigation, we discovered an internal Ford document stating that the decision had been made to "throw Firestone under the bus." They had done quite a good job of it.

For months, we tried to stay above Ford's attacks, focusing on Lampe's simple but brilliant campaign called "Making It Right," a campaign designed to win back our customers' faith in our company and our products. The thrust of the campaign was that we would do whatever it took to right our wrongs and win back our customers' trust. But after many months of attempting to absorb Ford's volleys, we decided to fight back.

In an internal meeting, several of us urged that we fire Ford as a customer, which in turn would free us to tell the world what we had learned about the stability issues on certain models of the Explorer. Lampe agreed with the recommendation, informed Japan of our decision, and we loaded our cannons.

A few days later, we publicly announced that we were terminating our 100-year relationship with the Ford Motor Company, a relationship that was forged by Henry Ford and Harvey Firestone in the early 1900s. We were Ford's largest tire supplier and Ford was our largest single customer. Harvey Firestone's granddaughter had even married Henry Ford's grandson. Their son, William Clay Ford, Jr., was the presiding

---

[4] Adam L. Penenberg, *Blood Highways: The True Story behind the Ford-Firestone Killing Machine* (Wayzgoose Press, 2012).

chairman of the Ford Motor Company. It was more than business, it was, in some ways, family. But that storied relationship was now over.[5]

We came out fighting. We told the public why we believed certain models of the Ford Explorer had stability issues. This was backed up by tests that were performed by one of the world's leading automotive engineers. Our message was tires fail on occasion (although it happens with much less frequency now than it did several decades ago). That is a fact of life. But cars should be able to pull over, not roll over. We coupled this with ads in which the great Mario Andretti praised the benefits of Firestone tires both on and off the racetrack. Critically, our employees and independent tire dealers began to take pride in our organization again. Most importantly, the tables began to turn.

Ford's reaction was swift. It held a televised press conference in which it announced that it was voluntarily removing millions of additional Firestone tires from all its SUVs and pickup trucks, claiming they were unsafe. Many thought that would be our death. If Ford didn't have faith in any of our tires, how could the public. But some of us saw it differently. Ford had overplayed its hand. There was no data, no basis whatsoever, for Ford to suddenly remove about 13 million tires from its vehicles other than as revenge for firing our cannons at Ford and the Explorer.

With this announcement, Congress called for a new set of hearings, some 10 months after we had announced the initial tire recall. It was Jacques Nasser versus John Lampe. Unquestionably, after hours of Congressional hearings, Lampe came out on top. He was quick in his replies and completely authentic, almost like a choirboy. Credible, articulate, and humble. Nasser, by comparison, was defensive and cantankerous. The tables had turned, or at least the playing field had leveled.

---

[5] Some years later, during my tenure as CEO of Bridgestone Americas, we resumed tire tales to Ford.

The public began to see Bridgestone in a new light, and unfortunately for Nasser, they saw Ford in a new light as well. As Ford's costs skyrocketed by replacing millions of Firestone tires, its war chest dwindled. Not too long thereafter, Nasser was removed from the company. The litigation tables also began to turn. Rather than plaintiffs' focusing solely on us, they had another object in their scopes – Ford, claiming that the Explorer was defectively rollover prone. The cost of settling lawsuits, while still placing great stress on Bridgestone's bottom line, became more manageable as Ford began to share more of the burden.

Ultimately, despite the pundits' warnings, the company survived the recall. A few years after the recall was announced, the federal criminal grand jury investigation into the company's conduct closed without any indictments – a huge vindication. The class action cases and the state attorneys general investigation settled on favorable terms. We were still slogging our way through hundreds of personal injury cases, but we could see the light at the end of the long, very dark tunnel we had found ourselves in.

But the financial costs were huge. We were massively in debt from the recall and the income from business operations alone could not pay off that debt. That is where the Japanese taxpayer came to our rescue. Under Japanese law, the parent company could take a tax write off against significant parts of our debt, essentially allowing us to avoid restructuring.

Lampe was the hero, he was loved, and he was in charge. But he was exhausted from the stress and strains of saving the company, and so he retired in 2004, just as Bridgestone Americas was pulling itself from the grave.

The company then went about the process of rebuilding its business. It was tough going to be sure. The Firestone brand had been damaged, both in terms of reputation and sales. Over the next few years, the company's financials slowly improved, certainly not as quickly as any of us would have liked, but probably more quickly than we had any right to expect.

But then came the Great Recession of 2008. Like just about every company in the world, and certainly every major tire manufacturer, sales plummeted and so did profits. In early 2010, I was appointed as the CEO of Bridgestone Americas. With my appointment, the message was clear. Bridgestone Americas' parent company and its global shareholders wanted even better results.

I knew one thing for certain. The company would not significantly improve its financials by doing what it had been doing. Rather, if the financials were to dramatically improve, things had to change dramatically. And that is exactly what happened.

3

Recognizing a Need for Change

WESTERN UNION IS among the world's largest money transfer companies. But money transfer was not part of the company's original business. Samuel Morse sent the first telegram in 1844. A rush of entrepreneurs attempted to capitalize on the new communication technology. Western Union arose not long thereafter as the dominant telegraph company in the country. At its peak in 1929 the company sent 200 million telegrams. That business was entirely wiped out, however, by the internet. But Western Union branched off into other business over the years. One such business was money transfer, which continues strongly to this day.

Other companies have reinvented themselves from time to time. American Express started as a delivery service in 1850. The American Express credit card was not introduced until the 1950s. Today, it is a global credit card and travel services company.

Yet other companies failed to adopt to changing technology or consumer preferences. Polaroid, the camera and film company, reached its peak revenues in 1991. Ten years later it filed for bankruptcy. Some 80 million people used Blackberry at one point. Today, it's hardly a blip in the marketplace. Xerox failed to adapt to the digital world, instead believing that its copying machines would reign supreme. Yahoo focused on growing its media business rather than on its search engine. It even passed on an opportunity to buy Google and later to buy Facebook.

All of this begs the question of when should a leader drive change? Often times, a company's financial performance can beckon the need for change. Its revenues or profits are declining or perhaps competitors are simply outperforming the company in sales or other key metrics. These can be warning signs that something is amiss. Something needs to change.

Sometimes change is thrust upon an organization. Such was the case with the recent COVID pandemic, which pushed employees to work remotely and restaurants to focus on take out. The rise of the automobile beckoned the demise of the horse-drawn carriage. And so, Harvey Firestone adeptly transformed his business from carriage wheels to automobile tires.

Other times the need for change can be more subtle or even brought about by a company's own innovations. Steve Jobs faced just such a situation. While the iPhone was not the world's first smart phone, it was far and away its most successful. The iPhone became an appendage to our lives, and because of its innovative capabilities it is largely responsible for the fact that there are roughly 6.7 billion smart phones in use across the world. Staggering when you consider that the world's population is roughly 7.7 billion. Few can compare their results to what Steve Jobs achieved and Apple continues to achieve.

Among the many hard decisions Jobs had to make during his career was a particularly sticky one while developing the iPhone. At the time, Apple's single most popular product was the iPod, a small device that could store thousands of songs in the palm of your hand. Apple sold nearly 55 million of these remarkable little devices in 2008, up from about a half million just six years earlier. At its peak in sales, the iPod accounted for roughly 40 percent of Apple's revenue.

The question for Jobs was whether the iPhone would cannibalize the iPod's capability for storing and playing music. That is, should the iPhone be built with essentially the same capabilities that the iPod offered, plus the additional capabilities that the iPhone brought to the table? If the answer was yes, it might well drive the iPod's sales to near zero. If it did not, the success of the iPhone might not have been nearly as great. Mr. Jobs's answer: Yes. Cannibalize the iPod.

Other organizations have faced similar decisions with their core business, yet they could not overcome the issue at hand. Kodak could not pull off moving to digital and away from its leading traditional film products. Blockbuster could not see the future that streaming movies would replace renting VHS.

Steve Jobs was different than most leaders, and perhaps that was why he was so successful. He decided that the iPhone should have all the capabilities of the iPod, and with it he essentially doomed Apple's largest selling product. But the decision to cannibalize the iPod's capabilities was integral to Apple's long-term success as it was integral for propelling Apple to be one of the largest and most successful companies in the world.

The question remains. When should a leader drive change, whether it be for an entire company, a division, or even a department? Knowing when to change, whether it be products, culture, business strategy, key operating systems, or whatever the case may be, and deciding upon the nature of the change is perhaps a leader's greatest, and most difficult, responsibility. As the enormously successful Jack Welch said, "Change before you have to."

The answer, I believe, is that truly great leaders – the ones that become legends – have enormous vision. They are bold enough to envision a company that most others simply cannot see or if others can see it, they have the courage and will to drive that vision to a reality where others do not. And so, it took an Alan Mullaly to save the Ford Motor Company. He envisioned a company with better products and an entirely different culture than what had existed at the time. Lou Gerstner's force of will and vision allowed him to transform IBM from a computer company to a consulting giant.

GE achieved enormous success under Jack Welsh's leadership. He certainly did not shy away from change. Indeed, he changed the people, the culture, and the vision to being first or second in every market in which it participated. He sold those parts of the organization that were unlikely to achieve that market position and invested heavily in other profitable businesses that would. It worked. Welsh's advice, "change before you have to," is certainly worthy of great consideration.

* * *

Both the need for, and nature of, change can be influenced significantly by the stage of the organization's life cycle. There are at least four distinct phases in an organization's life cycle, each with their different challenges and need for change.[1] A start-up involves taking a business idea – whether creating a new product or service or entering an existing market such as selling computers or providing a service such as hair styling, dentistry, or car repairs – and turning it into a business. Business plans, products and services, and processes are being put in place, and much if not all of this must be tweaked or changed, sometimes often, to make the business work. A new company must be flexible to meet the demands of the marketplace or the risks of failure increase.

If a start-up organization survives, and according to the Small Business Administration only about 10 percent do, they move

[1] Some authorities have identified five stages of organization development: birth, growth, maturity, decline, and revival. For our purposes here, we are using four cycles, but the fundamental points in this book are not changed by either approach.

into the growth phase. In this phase there might be more customers or demand than the company can keep up with – certainly the kind of problem companies want to have. This, too, is a period of change. Processes need to be improved, more people hired, supply chains expanded, and capacity increased.

Once growth is established and processes are in place the organization enters the expansion phase, hopefully a phase of great financial results and success. Executives should be evaluating how to expand the business, such as more and different offerings to customers or taking current offerings to new customers in new geographies. But this also is the stage where a leader can get too comfortable, and they might miss opportunities for new business avenues or a very important indicator that significant change is required if the current success is to continue.

Once markets are saturated, competition is fierce, and product sales have peaked or started to decline, an organization transitions to the fourth stage, referred to as the maturity stage. This is the stage where change is essential to avoid significant decline. That change can take many forms, including the possibility of exiting the market.

Bandag was the largest tire retreader in the world. It was headquartered in Iowa, and it built a global tire retreading franchise business. Tire retreading became a very important part of cost control for most large trucking fleets. When a tire's tread was worn out, it often could be retreaded, and the tire's carcass could be used at least once and perhaps more. Bandag had fiercely maintained its independence from the major tire companies, asserting that its retreading process worked on each of the major tires in the marketplace.

Over time, the major tire companies – Michelin, Goodyear, Continental, and Bridgestone – saw a potential business opportunity and they each got involved in the retreading business in one form or another. This became a threat to Bandag's vast business. Marty Carver, Bandag's owner, ultimately decided that rather than waiting for the fierce competition with the major tire companies to sort itself out over many years and with the increasing possibility that Bandag's business could be substantially reduced or even at risk, the wiser strategy was to sell.

That strategic decision was a huge change for the organization and was necessitated by the growing maturity of the retreading business. And so, in 2007, Bridgestone bought Bandag. If Carver had put off the decision for some time, it is likely shareholders would have suffered, as Bandag's value likely would have declined because of the increasing competition from the major tire companies.

* * *

The bottom line is change is the order of the day. Therefore, knowing how to successfully make changes is of prime importance. The Six Lessons of Change are essential if the desired changes are to work.

In the start-up, growth, and expansion stages, everything is new, and everything is constantly changing and evolving to make the business work and grow. In the maturing stage, organizations typically meet a critical juncture to either change or become irrelevant. Such changes can involve major organizational, strategic, and cultural decisions and the changes can be massive undertakings.

Organizational and governance issues can result in inefficiencies or poor decisions. Poor hiring decisions, poor investment decisions, and the wrong market strategy are among the many other things that can go wrong in business.

A toxic culture can do the same, as well as drive the strongest members of the team to seek employment elsewhere. Indeed, McKinsey studied 1,000 companies and concluded that those with a positive culture obtain a 60 percent higher shareholder return than those with an average culture and a 200 percent better return than those with a poor culture.[2] Poor cultures can occur in start-up or very mature companies.

The challenge for management is to periodically take a step back and objectively look at the organization, its financials, the market, and particularly its company culture, and imagine what the organization could be.

Often, it can be difficult for a leader to recognize that there is a need for change. But recognizing the need for change and then envisioning something different is a leader's greatest calling. To assist in that regard, below are some of these key indicia that change is likely in order.

Stagnation

Industries often become stagnant or experience low growth.[3] In any given year due to a variety of circumstances, growth may exceed the long-term trend of negative or slight growth, but that blip in the trend is only a temporary mask on the reality of stagnation. That is the reality of life, or should we say, the marketplace. Supply eventually meets demand, even with products that were once high growth. As an industry becomes stagnant it is easy to fall into a rut.

---

[2] Carolyn Dewar and Reed Doucette, "Culture: 4 Keys to Why It Matters," McKinsey Organization Blog, https://www.mckinsey.com/business-functions/people-and-organizational-performance/our-insights/the-organization-blog/culture-4-keys-to-why-it-matters.

[3] Stagnation can have different definitions, but generally it refers to an industry experiencing long-term negative growth or significantly less growth than an objective measure such as GDP. See Richard G. Hamermesh and Steven B. Silk, "How to Compete in Stagnant Industries," *Harvard Business Review*, September 1979. In stagnant industries, growth often requires capturing market share from competitors rather than from simply meeting high growth demand.

Certainly, one of the most obvious signs of stagnation is a company's financial performance. Slow growth in sales and shrinking margins are, of course, tell-tale signs that an industry is mature and that a company could be stagnant. Other signs are intense competition to obtain higher sales, much of which comes at the expense of one or more competitors.

There also can be signals within a company that it is stalling out or struggling. A company has established its place in the market and, whether expressly or implicitly, essentially becomes content, or at least unable to see a way out of, the status quo. The executive team could develop the mentality that the company is what it is. For example, maybe it's a follower rather than the leader in its industry. In some cases, this can be a legitimate business strategy or it can be a resignation to stagnation.

Indeed, a CEO I talked with after my retirement said that a member of his team was convinced the company could never be the true leader in its respective industry. That company was in a fiercely competitive industry, struggling to make even the slightest gains in market share and fighting hard to prevent the competition making inroads into its customer base. The organization had fallen into a rut, doing the same thing every day and every year that it did the day and the year before. It lost the ability to imagine a different future than what it currently had.

Such an attitude would have been a complete anathema to both Harvey Firestone and Shojiro Ishibashi, who founded their respective companies on the concept of new ideas. Mr. Firestone said, "Capital isn't that important in business. Experience isn't that important. You can get both of these things. What is important is ideas."[4] With that mantra, among the countless Firestone technological and business innovations were raised tire treads (like we have today) for improved traction, "gum-dipped" tires for greater strength and resistance to heat, pneumatic tires for tractors for greatly improved performance, and, in 1926, an

---

[4]"35 Marvelous Harvey Firestone Quotes," brandongaille.com.

ambitious nationwide network of Firestone tire and automotive service stores, known today as Firestone Complete Auto Care. That history of innovations and excellence continues with today's Bridgestone. The company invented the remarkable Blizzak snow tire, which redefined the winter tire market, and it manufactures the industry leading run-flat tires (tires which continue to perform even after losing their air pressure).

Perhaps one reason that mature companies become stagnant is they really don't push themselves. New ideas aren't encouraged or rewarded; rather, such companies are slogging their way through each day trying to preserve their piece of the pie and take a tiny bite out of someone else's. As is the case so often in life, one gets what they expect, and if a company doesn't expect new ideas, it is unlikely to get them.

Further, if a company suffers from a top-down, command-and-control culture, new ideas are unlikely to surface. Such a culture discourages employees from speaking up, particularly with bold and novel ideas.

I recently talked to a friend who had joined Amazon. The friend said that when she interviewed with Amazon she was asked what new business opportunities Amazon should be considering. Imagine that. A person who had never worked for or with the company for even one minute was asked what new profit center Amazon – one of the most successful companies in history – should consider. She ultimately was hired by Amazon, and a significant part of her periodic review is what new business ideas she brings to the table.

Amazon is building, or perhaps has built, a process to fight stagnation. It is a process to keep the company growing, profitable, and vibrant. Perhaps that is one of the reasons why Amazon's market cap exceeds $1.5 trillion as of this writing. You get what you expect.

Some innovative companies have the motto of "fail fast, fail often." Explore many new innovations, decide before spending huge amounts of time and money if an idea will work (both technologically and in the market), and if not, move on to the next idea. That's how a company finds the relatively few gems that have big impacts, so the theory goes.

That motto, or mottos with similar import, is not part of a stagnant company's lexicon. Rather, a stagnant company plows ahead, doing what it has done for years. Perhaps that is why the executive referred to above thought his company could never be the true leader in its industry.

* * *

Another sign of stagnation is when a company builds a strong and nearly impenetrable fortress-type wall around itself. That is, the company simply does not let the outside in. Two ways to bring new ideas to the table are through good consultants and hiring from the outside. In some stagnant companies, consultants are taboo; hiring from the outside – that is, lateral hires – is a rarity, at best.

In a stagnant company, management often believes that consultants can offer little but take an enormous amount (that is, the high rates they can charge). Moreover, consultants are not to be trusted; they have an agenda – that is, to make money. Of course, there is some truth to that high-quality consultants can bring fresh ideas, perspectives, and processes to the table. Indeed, many of the most successful companies in the world use consultants regularly and to great effect. Indeed, the right consultant, like the right doctor, the right lawyer, or the right executive, can add significant value.

At Bridgestone Americas, we worked closely with the Hay Group to redefine the company's culture. We also worked with the Boston Consulting Group to help drive organization and operational efficiencies. But such things rarely happen in most stagnant companies.

Stagnant companies also often refrain from hiring middle or senior level talent from the outside. Bringing in executives from other companies is another way to bring new ideas to the table, but in some companies, it is frowned upon. The outsider doesn't know the industry or the business and so it would be too difficult and time consuming to educate a new executive and get that individual up to speed on the ins and outs of the business. Moreover, an executive from the outside would be an unknown entity. Better to pick someone internal, who, by the way, will likely continue doing what had always been done. What such a company usually gets is a continuation of the same thinking that has perpetuated the stagnation in the first place.

A company that builds walls around itself cannot have visibility to what other organizations are doing, especially outside their industry. Excellent consultants and wise hiring from the outside with some regularity can bring that visibility to the conference rooms where significant decisions are made. This allows for better decisions and new ideas, which can help overcome stagnation. Without such visibility, however, mature companies are almost certainly going to evolve right into a rut, and that rut is not likely to serve the organization well in the long run.

* * *

Yet another sign of stagnation can be a company's processes. Markets evolve as do technologies and customers. A vibrant company recognizes that its business processes need to evolve with the times. A stagnant company, however, often does not, and over time the business suffers.

A company's processes can, of course, greatly impact customer satisfaction. Recently, a family member ordered some clothes online. When the order was placed the vendor electronically estimated that the clothes would arrive in about two weeks. Nine days later, the vendor notified my family member that the clothes were sold out and so the order could not be filled. The family member accordingly canceled the order. About a week later, clothes were delivered from the vendor even though the order had been canceled. Perhaps not surprisingly, the clothes that were delivered were the wrong ones and the wrong sizes.

It is possible that this was a one-off, a complete anomaly for this vendor. But more likely it wasn't. There was so much wrong with the vendor's processes that it is hard to imagine its fill-rate (the percent of the orders that are filled correctly and timely) was very good. As a result, it is likely leaving money on the table and losing business largely because of its poor processes. If that is the case, its processes need to be changed, and it is also a warning light that the company is stagnant and in need of significant change.

Lifetime Employment

In a few contexts, lifetime employment can be a very good thing, and not just for the person who is the direct recipient of being employed for life. Such is the case, for example, for federal judges in the United States, also known as Article III judges. They are nominated by the president and confirmed by the Senate. Under Article III of the Constitution, they cannot be removed while in office except through impeachment by the House of Representatives and then conviction by the Senate. Such removals are extraordinarily rare; indeed, it has happened only eight times in our country's history. Nor can a federal judge's pay be reduced while in office. A pretty decent gig if you can get it.

The benefit of this system is that it insulates judges from the emotions, pressures, and possible recriminations of the majority and of politicians. Thus, the United States Supreme Court is free to strike down laws passed by Congress and signed by the president as unconstitutional even when the Congress and president vehemently disagree. Similarly, the high court has invalidated state laws creating "separate but equal" schools and other public facilities despite the fury of large segments of the population that feared black and white people being in the same school or restroom. More recently, every United States

Supreme Court justice appointed by President Trump ruled against him in his efforts to overturn the 2020 presidential election. Without life tenure, these and many other great judicial decisions that have helped define our country and preserve the rule of law almost certainly would not have been possible. In some situations, life tenure can serve the greater good.

So much for Civics 101. In most other contexts, and certainly in a place of business striving to thrive in the competitive world, lifetime employment is usually not a very sound policy. While few, if any, companies expressly subscribe to the concept of lifetime employment, some organizations operate that way.

I have talked with executive after executive, and in other contexts I so often hear a similar song. Their organizations generally fire people who steal from the company or do something illegal. But they all too often set a relatively low bar for performance, and so, weak performers stay with the organization.

Rather than making the tough decision about someone whose performance is not up to snuff, some companies tolerate the substandard work. Sometimes, the poor performer will be moved to a different part of the organization. The move isn't because it was a better fit for that person's talents, but because it was deemed easier than dealing directly with the person's performance. Of course, the team that hired the underperformer often has little or no idea that the person wasn't performing in their prior position. After a period of time – perhaps years – of disappointing performance in the new position, that person might well be moved again. In some organizations it can be a repeating cycle.

Performance reviews were required, the executives reassured me. The purpose of the reviews, of course, was to give the employee feedback so they could alter, and hopefully improve, their performance. But they said some executives didn't always tell people if their performance was unsatisfactory. And so, the tough conversations that are part of a manager's responsibilities might not happen.

Further, several executives I have talked with admitted that they or their colleagues sometimes either weren't honest with many about their performance or they didn't set their standards for performance high enough. Some managers, I was told, rarely indicated a poor performance or a needs improvement rating. Instead, someone who was underperforming would receive a satisfactory rating, which, of course, reinforced the weak performance. What's more, colleagues almost always know that individual was underperforming; the manager's failure to deal with the situation demotivates them and might even cause some to reduce their work effort. Why should they put in the extra effort if a weak performer doesn't have to?

Often, I would ask the executives who shared these stories if their company was overperforming or underperforming. Almost always the response was the same: underperforming. Coincidence? Probably not.

Of course, those companies had their stars and superstars. Those individuals were particularly driven or competitive and their personal constitution simply would not allow them to give anything but their best all of the time. Those were the ones who got promoted, and understandably so.

But for some stagnant companies, if you go to work regularly, work at a relatively decent pace, and don't steal from the company, you are pretty much golden, at least in terms of the risk of losing your job.

In the case of federal judges, lifetime appointments allow them to do their job without fear of recrimination so they can make the tough decisions. When this happens in business it is the opposite. Some, perhaps many, people will not rise to the occasion and perform at their highest level unless the system and the manager compels them to. They will "hide" somewhere in the organization and not do a lot more than just show up. When this happens, the company misses out on their energy, their talent, and their ideas.

Those companies get what they tolerate. If someone doesn't self-motivate, the company accepts the performance level they offer. Perhaps not quite the same as the life tenure of federal judges, but close enough. But for some, a pretty decent gig if you can get it.

Command and Control

Many issues need the CEO's attention. But many issues do not, and in a well-run company most issues should never reach the CEO's desk. By way of example, Bridgestone Americas had a suite at the Bridgestone Arena, home of the NHL team the Nashville Predators, and the venue of countless music and other events in "Music City." The main purpose of the suite was to entertain customers. It doesn't take a rocket scientist to know that the CEO should not be deciding the menu to be served when customers were in the suite. Even though the decision may not take much time, others had the responsibility to handle those particular decisions.

In another example, Bridgestone Americas owned a small Learjet, an essential tool for executives to efficiently get to our many out-of-the-way manufacturing plants and other facilities in places like Wilson County, North Carolina. Indeed, without the jet, it could take a full day of travel time to get to some of our plants, and a full day to get back, and that assumes commercial flights did not have significant delays or cancellations. With the company jet, it would take an hour or less. It was incredibly efficient, so much so that we called it our time machine. As one can imagine, there was great demand for using the jet because it saved so much travel time. We got maximum value out of the jet by using it as opposed to it sitting on the ground. An issue we faced though was which executives could use the jet for any given trip they had planned.

One person asked me if I, as CEO, should decide who can use the jet and when. I declined the opportunity. While that might be a somewhat more complex decision than what food and drink to serve when entertaining customers in the suite at the Bridgestone Arena, the CEO is not a travel agent. That simply wouldn't be the highest and best use of the CEO's time. Instead, I asked the controller to develop and adopt guidelines for the jet's use, and the responsibility for overseeing the program was assigned to an individual within the controller's team.

The point is there can be a tendency for some leaders to be top-down. Some people call this command and control. That is, most decisions were made at the top, by the top. When carried to an extreme, this could even include what wine gets served when entertaining customers in the company suite.

To some, perhaps, that sounds like the way things should be done. The senior most person should make the decisions. If top-down decision-making is the hallmark of an organization, however, that is a strong sign that things must change, and in a big way.

It may have worked and been appropriate in the past, but in today's extraordinarily complex world, no one person can have all the answers. In fact, in a well-run, talented organization, particularly a sizable organization, effective leaders rely heavily on the knowledge, experience, and ideas of others to make the best decisions for the organization. Indeed, sales executives, for example, are much closer to the action than the CEO is and so they are almost always better positioned to make sales-related decisions.

If a senior executive is making too many decisions, then the people below her are not earning their pay. They are not, in effect, doing their job. Rather, the senior executive is doing it for them. Similarly, the senior executive is down in the weeds, and not spending her time on the bigger issues where a greater difference can be made, and where others cannot and should not make decisions.

Moreover, when the senior executive makes the decisions, people below her are not responsible for the outcomes. If the decision goes south, it is easy for the more junior person to say it wasn't their fault; all they did was follow directions, and they are right. Not letting others make decisions and handle the associated outcomes also stunts growth and jeopardizes the long-term leadership capabilities of a company.

Some people might prefer a boss who uses a command-and-control leadership style. It takes the responsibility off them. Life can be easy that way. No responsibility, no personal risk. But a leader must ask themselves, are those really the kind of people you want working in the company? Are those the kind of people who are going to excel and help take the company to the next level?

Finally, and perhaps most important, a good leader wants their team to be fully engaged, taking responsibility, and making things happen. If the senior executive is making all the decisions, the junior executive becomes disengaged, doesn't feel valued and appreciated, and is reluctant to act on their own. As important, the company moves slowly and continuous improvement is sacrificed as it waits for one person to make decisions, and especially when the decisions are made by someone removed from the action.

Steve Jobs said, "It makes no sense to hire smart people and tell them what to do; we hire smart people so they can tell us what to do."[5] If a person needs to be micromanaged as a matter of course (other than in a training situation), the problem is clear. They are not the right person for the job. Similarly, if an executive or manager cannot refrain from micromanaging capable people, he is probably not the right person for the job either.

Certainly, major decisions should be made at the top. In a typical year, there are relatively few such decisions. Driving change to excel in the future, acquisitions and spinoffs, fundamental

---

[5] Marcel Schwantes, "Steve Jobs Once Gave Some Brilliant Management Advice on Hiring Top People. Here It Is in 2 Sentences," *Inc.*, Oct. 17, 2017.

business performance issues and strategies, governance and organizational structure, major HR policies and issues such as executive performance and significant personnel changes, corporate culture, board and major shareholder issues, and major operational issues are most of the key things that should consume a CEO's time. Conversely, ordinarily, a CEO of a large organization should not spend much time on most of the daily issues that come up in every sizeable organization.

A command-and-control culture has resounding consequences – and often not for the best. One executive of a company I talked with told me how his company had a "shoot first, aim later" approach. He shared that a senior executive came up with the idea of making a large investment in a foreign country. That executive was convinced it was the right thing to do. The executive put together a team to confirm that the investment made sense and would have an acceptable payback or return on the investment.

The executive was known for being intolerant of answers that didn't confirm his opinion. So, no surprise, the analysis predicted that there would be a strong return on the investment because the country in question was going to experience very significant economic growth and prosperity for many years to come, and with that the demand for the company's product would accordingly grow substantially, allowing the company to set a relatively high price for its product.

But the analysis proved wrong. There was the anticipated economic growth in the beginning, but it did not last. The demand for the high-end product didn't materialize. The investment, in the fullness of time, was a bust.

At the end of the day, the reason for the poor decision was the organization's top-down, command-and-control culture. Dissenting voices could not be heard, a truly objective evaluation, one in which contrary scenarios were fully considered, simply was not possible because management would not hear of it.

The culture at that company did not enable others to critically scrutinize ideas from the top, to question their wisdom, objectively analyze the data, think through the potential problems, develop alternatives for consideration, and overcome any biases in management's understanding of the facts and predictions about the future.

A sure sign that a culture needs serious and immediate change is when there is a great overriding deference to seniority. That is, true debate and discussion, deep objective analysis, critically challenging the ideas of someone more senior is taboo.

In some companies, when the person at the top has a direction in mind that is the end of the story. Discussion is cut off. The data is interpreted in a way that supports the predetermined inclinations – something experts call "decision bias," which is a bias in the decision-making process for many people and companies. Fait accompli. That is a formula for poor decisions that may ultimately lead to a company's demise.

Silos

Another significant impediment to organizations is that they can become "siloed." Silos are where the right hand and the left hand aren't on the same page. In a corporate context, for example, if the sales team pushes one product but manufacturing makes a different product, that's a problem.

The larger and more mature an organization, the more prone it is to operate in silos. It is a battle many companies must constantly fight. Often, the problems are not intentional. Each part of the organization can be so busy or perhaps so caught up in the day-to-day work that its communication with other parts of the organizations may be lacking. Other times, there can be a lack of trust between departments or the reward structure may not incentivize communication and collaboration.

Take tires, for example. Tires seem like pretty simple black, round pieces of rubber. Really, that couldn't be further from the truth. Tires, themselves, and the broader tire business, are extremely complex. Tires are highly engineered, advanced pieces of technology often composed of roughly two dozen different components. The exact composition, construction, and size of each of those components often varies by the type and by the size of tire that is being made. Those components often are not interchangeable.

Every year Bridgestone produced tens of millions of tires. Of those, there are thousands of different types and sizes of tires. Having the right raw materials in the right quantity and the right place at the right time to produce the many components in each of the thousands of different tires in our various plants is a mind-boggling undertaking.

After producing the right tire, in the right quantity and at the right time, then the company must manage a complex inventory with several thousand SKUs. Then it's a matter of getting the exact right tire to the right car, truck, or tractor assembly plant, for example, or to the many different wholesale and sometimes thousands of different retail locations across the country, again all at the right time. It is all remarkably complex. And all of that must be well-coordinated with sales and marketing.

For all this to work well the different parts of the organization need to coordinate and communicate openly and often. Tire development, manufacturing, purchasing, supply chain management, distribution, marketing, and sales must be on the same page.

The complexity in the tire business extended to the tire development process as well. It generally takes three to five years to develop new truck tires. Truck tires, for example, need to be tested and retested in the real world to ensure they will perform as expected under incredible stresses and strains in a variety of conditions.

Adding to the complexity, some truck tires are designed for the steer axle, others for the drive axle, and others for the trailer positions on the 18-wheeler. And, of course, there are many different types of trucks requiring different types of tires. Imagine if the tire development group developed a new drive tire when what the sales group needed was a new steer tire. That can happen in a siloed company, and it would be a disaster.

Silos are, in all likelihood, a product of human nature. A person and department or group has their territory or area of expertise. Survival instincts push that person or group or department to keep others out: "We know what's best, we will do it our way, and your input isn't welcome." Anyone outside of the group might be considered a threat. To a certain degree, it's self-preservation.

Silos can be a product of organizational structure. No organizational structure is perfect. Each has its advantages and disadvantages. A straight hierarchical organization creates clear lines of authority and helps identify redundancies. But it can also inhibit collaboration and encourage a territorial mindset.

Many years ago, large companies tended to organize themselves into smaller pieces to improve manageability and focus. Bridgestone Americas did this as well in the early 1990s, and it was of great benefit in helping to integrate the Bridgestone and Firestone organizations. In so doing, tire manufacturing, distribution, and each other part of the business became their own "organization." This was the right structure for the company at the time.

But, over the years and as the company grew, communications and efficiencies were not always optimized. The various companies within the larger Bridgestone Americas organization developed their own policies and processes that were good for them, but not always best for the broader organization. Over time, different parts of the organization developed their own HR groups, legal groups, IT groups, etc., and with that their own processes and policies. This helped their individual operations, but it ultimately created redundant cost structures. It also inhibited collective decisions that could benefit the company as a whole. By way of example, each part of the organization developed and negotiated their own cell phone policies with different carriers rather than the broader organization using its combined purchasing power to negotiate better terms with a single cell phone company.

To be sure, potential problems exist in just about any organizational structure. No structure is without its drawbacks. That is one reason why a company's culture is so important. A positive, fast-paced, open, and constructive culture can help overcome some of the inefficiencies in any organizational structure. But the organizational structure can also take on a life of its own, if you will, and drive the culture in unwanted directions.

At the end of the day, each organization must decide what structure is best for it, and it is likely that the structure will need to change over time as the company and its business changes.

But the bottom line is this: silos in any operation create inefficiencies. In addition to the increased cost, silos hinder an organization's ability to operate as effectively as it otherwise might. Silos are a tell-tale sign that there is a need for change.

It's Not Okay to Not Be Okay

One executive I met told me a story about the company he had worked for some years ago: the company had not been doing well, and it held an offsite meeting to discuss the various problems it had and to come up with a plan of attack to fix the key ills. This was the first time such a meeting had been held within the company.

The CEO, who also had founded the company many years prior, took enormous pride in his company. He had been successful, at least for a while, and was a strong-willed, emotional person. An outside consultant had been retained to facilitate the offsite meeting, and he strongly advised the CEO to watch and listen to the discussion, rather than actively participate. The fear was he would shut down fruitful discussion by his occasional mercurial outbursts.

The meeting had gone well. Toward the end of the day the group had identified several key issues where improvement was needed, and they had worked on a potential game plan to address the issues. There was positive energy in the room. The group was proud of what they had accomplished and began to feel a renewed sense of hope for the future.

But then things went south.

As the meeting was wrapping up, the CEO could hold back no longer. The story goes that he stood up, beet red, as his anger exploded into a scathing tirade. He began by saying he had been asked to sit silently, which he had done, but could do so no longer. He proceeded to chastise his team not for identifying problems in the meeting, but for allowing the problems to exist in the first place. How could everyone have gone about their jobs as if everything was okay when it wasn't? They should all be ashamed of themselves, he admonished. Everyone in the room felt small and regretted being honest about the company's issues. They felt like they had been set up, only to be shot down. They had opened up, made themselves vulnerable, freely discussed some of the company's biggest issues, all on the premise that it was safe to do so. But it wasn't.

The meeting ended shortly thereafter and little more was done to follow up on the various opportunities that had been collectively identified. The problems were swept back under the rug. According to the executive who told the story, one of the promising young stars in the organization later commented that she learned one thing: "Never speak up again."

Of course, the problem wasn't with this young executive. The problem lay at the feet of the person whose tirade instilled a sense of fear in everyone. The company had the opportunity to change its culture to a more open workplace where issues and ideas could be freely and safely discussed; a company that attempted to solve problems, rather than ignore or discount them. Instead, something snapped the other way – reinforcing the organizational norm where people's survival instincts pushed them to keep their heads down.

And so, the company continued to be a place where people pretended to be okay even though the company was not. As one might expect, the company's struggles continued, and the executive who shared the story ultimately left after finding a position at a more successful organization.

* * *

The ghost of Jacob Marley in the 1843 novel *A Christmas Carol* by Charles Dickens had an oppressive collection of balls and chains around his neck. So do some companies. Often, their culture does not allow for open, honest, authentic conversation around areas for continuous improvement. They are stuck in a rut, afraid to upset the status quo. While they might not be content, they are not prepared to make the bold decisions – personnel and strategic and otherwise – needed to start a new and uncertain path. Rather, they are focused on the day-to-day slugfest trying to squeeze one more sale than the competition in their fiercely competitive marketplace. Those are the Jacob Marley set of balls and chains for that company.

The reluctance to drive significant change is grounded in risk. While change might drive extraordinary results for the company, there is often fear that the change effort might fail in one or more ways and it could prove disastrous for the organization. Such change efforts usually fail, however, because management was not fully invested and determined to drive the change to ultimate success.

Such leaders are well-advised to remember the words of Alan Deutschman: "Change or die." Edwards Deming put it another way: "Change is optional; survival is not mandatory."

For change to succeed, there are six lessons, six elements, needed for success. It all begins with Leadership and Vision. It then requires Culture and People to support it. Without them, the changes cannot be fully Aligned and Executed. These are the six essential, inextricably linked keys to successfully driving change, and this applies in just about all situations – from start-ups to mature organizations.

In Part II we will discuss each of those critical keys to success, and in the context of each, many of the steps we took to turn Bridgestone Americas into an even higher-performing organization.

PART II

The Six Lessons for Change

4

A Prelude for Change

In September 2009, following a presentation I made to the Bridgestone Board in Japan on corporate governance, I was told that the current CEO for Bridgestone Americas would be retiring in early 2010. I was asked to assume the position of CEO upon his retirement. As the general counsel and chief compliance officer for Bridgestone Americas, I led the law department, which consisted of about 80 people and a multi-million-dollar budget, mostly for handling litigation against the company. Now, I was being asked to run a 55,000-person global company with nearly $11 billion in revenues.

Bridgestone Americas was not a perfect company. No company is. It consisted of good people who worked hard and who were ethical and who took great pride in giving to their communities. However, the company operated in a very mature, extremely competitive industry. For all industry participants, it was essentially a fistfight to eke out better performance than its competitors. It was tough going. But Bridgestone shareholders, like all shareholders, wanted even stronger returns. Because Bridgestone Americas was the single largest part of Bridgestone globally, that naturally meant it had to obtain stronger returns than it had been achieving.

So, I was asked to take the company to the next level. This is what chief executive officers are supposed to do, but that is no small task. Opportunities like that don't happen every day. So, I overcame my fear of failure, accepted the offer, and became the CEO of Bridgestone Americas in 2010. At the same time, the then leader of our Latin American operations was promoted to COO, and we formed a partnership forged in driving change.

Bridgestone's global CEO, Shoshi Arakawa, my new boss, had made it clear that our responsibility was to significantly improve Bridgestone Americas' financial performance. Among other things, he had made a commitment to Bridgestone's shareholders to improve Return on Assets (ROA) to 6 percent for the global organization,[1] and it was my responsibility to help him fulfill that commitment. To do that, Bridgestone Americas had to do more than make incremental improvements. The improvements had to be huge. Mr. Arakawa did not say what he thought needed to change to obtain his desired financial improvements. That, he said, was up to us. But that things had to change was clear to me if we were to have any hope of significantly improving shareholder returns.

But change isn't easy. According to some estimates, as much as 70 percent of corporate change efforts fail. The change efforts either do not get off the ground, take way too long and fall by the wayside, or they simply do not produce the desired results.

Change on an individual level is difficult; we know this from the many failed New Year's resolutions many of us have made. It's even more challenging on an organizational scale. A few courageous souls might see the virtues in change, but many others resist it, either because they won't change or (think they) can't. Change is often perceived as a threat to their jobs, their self-worth, their income, even though instinctively some may know that the

---

[1] Edwina Gibbs, "Bridgestone Aims for 80% Profit Boost in 5 Years," October 22, 2007, https://jp.reuters.com/article/us-bridgestone-plans-id UST2474720071022.

current status is not in their long-term best interests. Significant change is an uphill climb and does not happen overnight.

The American Renaissance man and one of our Founding Fathers, Ben Franklin, had it right when he opined there are three types of people: those who will never change, those who can be persuaded to change, and those who make change happen. Indeed, data suggests that a very small percentage would buy into our change efforts from the start, and that percentage might grow to about 15 percent. Also, roughly the same percentage of employees would likely never fully buy into the changes. Successful change efforts must, therefore, (1) persuade the middle 70 percent of employees to accept the changes, and (2) deal with those who simply can't or won't accept the changes. This was our challenge, against the odds, to move our 55,000 employees with us through the changes we needed to make to become a higher-performing organization.

Without a doubt change is hard, particularly cultural change. It takes enormous time, devotion, and persistence. It is not an overnight conversion but closer to an evolutionary process often measured over years. But in the fullness of time, we succeeded.

Having driven successful change at Bridgestone Americas for more than six fulfilling and exhausting years, it is clear to me that there are six lessons or elements to successfully driving change:

1. Leadership
2. Vision
3. Culture
4. People
5. Alignment
6. Focused Execution

These six lessons apply whether changing an entire company, a division, a team, or a function. The six lessons overlap and are intertwined. It will not suffice to do two or three or even five of them. Each is necessary. With these six lessons, combined with time (and it does take time) and persistence, the change is almost certain to be successful. Without addressing every one of the six lessons, the change effort will almost certainly fall short or fail entirely.

The hard part is sticking with it and overcoming the resistance. In the following chapters, we explore the six lessons for successfully driving change in detail and we describe how we – the management team working together – transformed an iconic giant, Bridgestone Americas, in the process.

5

Leadership: Lesson #1

"People buy into the leader before they buy into the vision."

— *John Maxwell*

ESTIMATES ARE THAT in the Battle of New York in 1776, the American revolutionary army's makeshift fighting force consisted of roughly 10,000 men. There may have been more of these devoted men, but many were ill from disease, didn't have weapons or ammunition, or even boots or sufficient clothing. The revolutionaries had some limited cannons, but no naval presence to impact the course of the battle, and lower New York is surrounded and intertwined by navigable waters.

The British, the greatest military and naval power in the world at the time, had as much as three times the number of men, and they were well-trained, well-armed, and battle tested. They also were supported by some 70 ships, including ships of the line and frigates, that filled the bay and rivers. Moreover, a large part of the New York population was loyal to the Crown and wanted no part of the effort to separate from Britain. To say the odds were overwhelming is a vast understatement.

In addition to the remarkably brave men who were serving in the Continental Army, the Americans had one other thing on their side: a small but extraordinary group of leaders. Most of them had little military experience, but several had studied war tactics and were fiercely determined to advance the cause. Of course, the man at the top of this group was George Washington himself, and he had surrounded himself with smart and capable men who advised him well.

The Americans lost the battle of New York resoundingly and Washington's mistakes in the battle are well-documented. But the revolutionary army survived against the vastly superior British forces and retreated down the Atlantic coast. Then, a few months later, on Christmas evening in December 1776, Washington famously led a few thousand men across the frigid Delaware River in the dead of night. The risky plan was made considerably more dangerous by icy waters and a severe winter storm with howling winds, sleet, and snow. But the surprise attack the following morning at Trenton proved successful, and was a pivotal point in the war.

Some historians say that Washington did not possess the genius of some of the other men involved in the revolution from Great Britain. Whether he did or not, he had other critical qualities. Having led the revolutionary army to success over the British empire, then serving as president of the Constitutional Convention where the US Constitution was fiercely debated and drafted, and then setting the norms for the executive branch as the first president of the United States, one could argue that he is among the greatest change leaders in our country's history.

Certainly, one of Washington's greatest attributes was trust. His integrity was beyond reproach, and he was trusted by his soldiers, those he led, and by the Continental Congress, to whom he reported. They had faith in him to pull off the impossible. He led his army forward against impossible odds with an air of contagious confidence. He understood his position and instinctively knew that he had to maintain the trust all had placed in him. And he performed magnificently.

Another of his great attributes was a propensity for action. To cross the Delaware River at night in a freezing December strom with a rag-tag army could have been a suicide mission. But it worked. He had taken other similarly bold actions. Earlier, during the Battle of Boston, in the dead of a freezing night he ordered his troops to move cannons atop a strategic hill (a nearly impossible operation) overlooking the British troops. When the British awoke the following morning, they realized they had been outflanked and withdrew from Boston in embarrassment, hardly firing a shot. Indeed, there were occasions when Washington's inner circle, his war council, had to dissuade him of plans that might have proved disastrous, and he had the ability to listen to others. But action was Washington's instinct.

Other great change leaders have had these two essential attributes – trust and a propensity for action. Mahatma Gandhi, Nelson Mandela, and Martin Luther King, Jr., are synonymous with trust. Abraham Lincoln the same. Yet they all had the courage to act. King and Gandhi did it through leading peaceful but overwhelming protests of civil disobedience. Lincoln, for example, fired his extremely popular most senior general, George McClellan, because the general, fearing defeat, would not take the offensive against the confederate forces. At one point, Lincoln asked McClellan, "If you won't use your army, may I borrow it."

There are thousands of books and articles on leadership. The theories of what makes a successful leader are abundant, to say the least. Leadership has been studied so much that Jim Collins, in his research leading up to the book *Good to Great*, told his research team not to come back with findings that it is the leaders who helped turn around the businesses they studied. The data, however, were irrefutable. The leader at the time of transformation did matter, and it mattered a lot. Put another way, successful change requires leadership. It is essential, a requisite for change.

There are a multitude of aspects to leadership. To achieve meaningful change, though, there are two essential qualities a leader must possess and exhibit above all. The first is *trust*. Effective leaders have several tools to build trust, including self-leadership, humility, and empathy. People will follow a leader they trust. They likely will not follow a leader who they do not trust – at least not willingly.

The second quality is a *propensity for action*. A propensity for action is a term I chose carefully. A leader must act, but often before doing so, reflection, debate, and options should be fully considered. Thus, I prefer the term propensity for action as opposed to simply action, as it conveys that action is the order of the day, but after full consideration of the wisdom of the particular action.

Of course, the action, the type of changes the leader seeks to make, must be directionally appropriate. But without action, the status quo remains the status quo.

Trust

Many people are naturally inclined to resist change. Sometimes it is an intellectual response. They honestly believe that the change in question is not in the organization's best interests. They might, for example, disagree with the wisdom of a merger or a decision to outsource part of the company's production. But such intellectual debates often are not at the root of major resistance to change.

Resistance to significant change is often an emotional response and that response is provoked by fear.[1] What will the restructuring mean for me? Will there be a place for me in the new world and will I be able to survive in that world? If the company outsources portions of its production today, will it outsource the remaining production tomorrow, and if so, what does that mean for my manufacturing job? If the company restructures to address a strategic need, will I like my new boss? Will the new boss like me? Will the restructuring work or could this be the beginning of the

---

[1] Steve Nguyen, "Reasons Why People Resist or Support Organizational Change," *Workplace Psychology*, February 1, 2017.

end of my job or even the company? Change begets uncertainty, uncertainty begets fear, and fear begets resistance, both passive and active.

A leader driving change reduces and counters fear with trust. The organization must have faith in the leader to, if you will, take them to the promise land. With that trust, many are almost certain to rally behind the leader. Without it, the fear takes on a life of its own.

Shortly after I took over in 2010, we initiated a review of business processes to streamline operations in the organization and also to send a message that things were going to change. Coincidentally, during this business review process, we installed electronic turnstiles in the lobby of the headquarter building to prevent strangers from going up the elevator and into our offices without an escort. This was initiated because a trespasser had recently entered the building, ascended the elevator to Bridgestone Americas' offices, and stole a few computers. It was easy for trespassers to do this as the building had no meaningful security in place at the time. The electronic turnstiles that we installed would sound an alarm if someone went through them without a valid office badge. By any objective standard, this was a reasonable step for us to take to protect our people and property.

Rumors spread, however, that the real purpose of the electronic turnstiles was to monitor our employees' comings and goings to draw conclusions about their work ethic. The rumor was that this information would then be used to evaluate who was not working hard, and those individuals would be let go as part of the business efficiency review process.

This was flatly untrue and baseless, but it nonetheless took hold. This falsehood was driven out of fear arising from our program to streamline operations and reduce costs, and it is testament to the fear that change can provoke.

Fear can be a great motivator. It also can be the poison arrow that kills change efforts. Resistance, of course, can be overt, but it is perhaps more likely to be subversive. Either way, resistance, at best, delays change efforts and, at worst, completely stalls them. If fear propels resistance to change, a leader must be able to earn trust to help drive change. For employees to follow a leader willingly and enthusiastically through change, therefore, a leader must create trust. Trust helps win the battle over fear, and it is essential for any leader driving change.

Trust can be both created and destroyed through a variety of ways. The entirety of a leader's character, values, ethics, actions, or lack thereof, and management style must convey that the leader is worthy of trust. Integrity, communication, self-leadership, humility, empathy, and walking the walk all impact trust. Just about everything a leader says and does, and does not do, either strengthens trust or weakens it. Some of the key influencers on trust are discussed in the following sections:.

1. Integrity as an Element of Trust

Of course, integrity, character, and honesty are foundational to trust. Being honest, but respectful, is critical for earning trust. A leader who lies does so at his own peril, for once credibility is gone, it is nearly impossible to recover. And make no mistake, most of the time people can tell when someone is lying. Even if they can't, sooner or later the truth will likely come out.

There are several compelling reasons for a leader to act legally, ethically, and morally at all times, not the least of which is it's the right thing to do, to avoid going to jail and potentially massive legal liabilities for the leader and the organization. The leader who operates unethically, immorally, or illegally announces to all concerned that he or she is not trustworthy. Indeed, how can someone trust another who lacks morality, ethics, and crosses the line of legality. How can such a person be trusted to lead the company through a great change vision? How can one trust that person's vision or trust that as the company changes and evolves, he will treat people fairly?

Some may think few will know about the questionable behavior, so it is worth the risk. That is wrong. It is extremely difficult to fully hide illegal or unethical behavior. Business involves too many pieces, too many complexities, too many people to effectively hide such transgressions. Whether it is financial improprieties, fraud of some sort, discrimination, harassment, or just treating people in an unethical or poor manner, sooner or later others will likely know. Sooner or later, someone will spill the beans, word will get out, things will go south, and the jig will be up.

Indeed, the record is abound with conspiracies that failed and could not be kept under wraps. Nixon with Watergate and Trump paying hush money to a porn star are certainly examples of how difficult it is to keep conspiracies under wraps in the political world. Conspiracies rarely succeed, despite all the conspiracy theories that seem to inform today's politics.

The same is true in the corporate world. Volkswagen could not keep its emissions shenanigans under cover. Some pharmaceutical companies have filed for bankruptcy protection because of their efforts to hide the addictive effects of opioids. In 1988, tobacco companies paid over $200 billion for their false campaign to conceal the effects of smoking. Arthur Anderson could not hide its document destruction effort to cover up its knowledge of the Enron scandal, leading to the firm's complete collapse. The news is replete with executives who were fired (rightly so) for sexual harassment. The list goes on.

Moreover, a leader who engages in such conduct reveals his true character to those around him. They talk. Rumors spread. Trust is gone.

Effective leaders build trust. They never put their credibility and, with it, their ability to lead on the line by lying, cheating, acting unethically or engaging in other such behaviors. They know the entirety of their behavior, their words, and their actions, is under constant scrutiny and that scrutiny will and does positively, or negatively, impact that trust.

If you cannot trust a person to tell you the truth, to stand up for you when called for and to treat you fairly, it is difficult to imagine following that person. This is particularly important in the context of driving change, which necessarily involves addressing the fears of an uncertain future. Trust is the foundation of leadership.

2. Effective Communication as an Element of Trust

Throughout any change effort a leader must communicate effectively and often with all levels of the organization. That communication can (and should) take different forms: in-person, videos, written, and so on. But such communications are key. Communication is how the organization knows the vision (discussed in the next chapter), the expectations, the progress, the setbacks, and the goals. If the organization at each level is to rally behind the changes, the communications must be frequent, clear, and understandable. That builds trust. Conversely, if communications are not clear and understandable, the communicator will not be trusted.

One of the tools we used to communicate the changes and progress on those changes, as well as to build trust, was through town hall meetings. These meetings were far from the most time-efficient way to communicate, but they were almost certainly the most effective. Teammates could not only hear but see and feel the power of our words and inflections. There is no equal for the effectiveness of in-person communications.

Moreover, to develop trust, I vehemently took the position that employees were free to ask any question they would like in town hall meetings. Literally any question at all. Our teammates had as much invested in the company as did the senior management team. They had as much right as anyone to know all we could reasonably share with them. Moreover, if we didn't have a good answer to a question, then the point behind the question probably had merit, and so we likely had to rethink our position.

Every town hall meeting had the same flow. They began with a presentation, and when we were finished, we moved to the question-and-answer portion. I always began the Q-and-A session with this opening: "Now, it's your turn to ask anything that is on your mind. There's just one rule. There are no rules. Everything is fair game." I meant it. And so, the Q&A began.

In one town hall meeting an employee asked me if I had gone through a new training program that was required for every other manager in the organization. It was a fair question. Embarrassed, but truthfully, I admitted I had not, but said the point was well-taken. I would go through the training and report back to that team when the training was complete. I did just that. If we required everyone else to go through training, I should too. By being truthful, and then completing the training, I ultimately enhanced my credibility and helped reinforce trust.

Trust is not just about being honest, but also creating an environment that welcomes all questions, including tough ones. At one of the first town hall meetings a brave young lady asked a very emotional and difficult question. She articulately challenged whether the efficiency program was appropriate at all, and especially whether the consultants we were using to help drive efficiencies were truly qualified to do so. When she asked the question, her voice quivered, and one could feel the oxygen being taken out of the room. The room became completely silent.

People thought she would be fired, that her career with the organization was finished. Instead, I thanked her for the very difficult question, and answered it, knowing the answer wasn't really what most had hoped to hear (that is, most hoped I would agree, remove the consultant, and end the program, which I did not do). An HR VP urged that I do more to reinforce this woman's courage and candor so others would know that tough questions are welcome. After the meeting, I asked the woman to come to my office to personally thank her for her courage and I gave her a handwritten note of gratitude for her question. The outcome of her asking the question buzzed around the organization. Instead of being fired, she was positively recognized. Small acts such as this began to build trust in my leadership and helped the organization understand they could ask anything, challenge everything.

While everyone might not always like our answers, the organization needed to know that the answers were as truthful as possible. When leaders get angry about the questions on peoples' minds it feeds fear. Instead, empathy, discussed below, helps calm the fear and develops trust.

I was asked by some on more than one occasion if we wanted to have questions planted in the town hall meetings. I was vehement that it would be completely inappropriate.

If it were to ever get out that questions were planted, the value of town hall meetings would be destroyed, as would our credibility. Moreover, however Pollyannaish it may sound, town hall meetings were the opportunity for employees to ask about their company and raise issues that were on their mind. They had every right to know as much about the company as the leadership team could reasonably share, for they were investing their livelihood in the company's future.

Of course, there is a difference between honesty and complete transparency. There are circumstances where a leader cannot be completely frank with everyone, such as when the company is in negotiations for an acquisition. The acquisition could be jeopardized if those discussions became public and, in some cases, federal law prohibits certain untimely disclosures.

Another difficult example might be if someone asks something to the effect that there are rumors of people cuts, a plant closure, or changes to the compensation or retirement plans. If there is no basis for such rumors it is easy to say exactly that, but the leader must be careful not to box themselves in should something come into play down the road. So, an appropriate answer might be, "The rumor is false. We are not considering any such thing. But I cannot say we will never consider a plant closure. That depends on many things like the plant performance and the market conditions."

More difficult is answering a question when there is a legitimate basis for the rumor, such as if meaningful changes to the compensation or retirement plans are, in fact, under consideration. A leader must be prepared to respond, but lying is never a good choice. A few options are, "If and when we have something to announce I will announce it. Right now, absolutely no decisions have been made on this topic." Or, "We are looking at our compensation strategy. That is part of our obligation to you and the shareholders to make certain our products and services are always competitive in the market and that our compensation programs allow us to both keep and attract talent to the organization. I have no idea if or when we will have anything to announce but if we do, I assure you it will be fair to all stakeholders."

These types of answers do not rule out that change might happen, and therefore they can provoke fear. But these answers also build rather than destroy trust. The answers might not always make people happy. While it may sound cold, such is life, if you will. Yet they will most likely believe that the answers are fair. If answers to tough questions are communicated in a way that describes the process by which the decisions are made and if they are delivered in an honest, sincere, and caring way, people might not like the answer, but they will start to understand it and trust is preserved.

Corporate speak is a sure-fire way to lose credibility and weaken trust. Words like "operationalize," "deliverable," and "synergize" usually add little if any value. Acronyms may be known to some, but usually are not clear to all. Many listeners must think about the acronym and what it really means. Such language is distracting at best, and often sufficiently obscure that others don't understand the real message. Rather than sounding sophisticated, it detracts from the honesty of the message.

One of my college professors said he heard students say that another professor was very smart, but they just couldn't follow what he was saying. Probably many have heard similar things from time to time. That professor then rhetorically asked how would you know someone is smart if you don't understand what he's saying? His point is well-taken.

Kate Cray of the *Atlantic* mocked corporate speak beautifully: "Got to tactically evaluate this strategic initiative from 40,000 feet before proving out whether it's going to upcycle productivity or negatively impact the cross-functional team members that are coordinating the multi-pronged approach to synergizing the year-over-year growth strategy."[2] No one is served well by corporate speak, least of all a leader. Avoid it at all costs.

It is much better to choose language that others throughout the organization both use and understand. If they understand what you are saying, and if it is substantively persuasive, they will buy into it, at least intellectually. If they don't understand you, then you have missed an opportunity to persuade key constituents and you've created mistrust.

3. Self-Leadership as an Element of Trust

By almost all accounts, Babe Ruth was the greatest baseball player who ever lived. Only a few players have surpassed his career 714 home runs, and he still holds the all-time record for slugging percentage. Although known as a slugger, he also had a remarkable .342 career batting average, tenth on the all-time list. But before becoming a position player so his lethal bat could be a factor in every game, he was a pitcher, and he could pitch very well. He won about two-thirds of his 150 starts, ninth best all-time, and he bragged a career 2.27 ERA, seventeenth best all-time. The Babe – the Great Bambino, the

---

[2] Kate Cray, "Something We Can All Agree On? Corporate Buzzwords Are the Worst," *The Atlantic*, May 5, 2020.

Sultan of Swat, the King of Crash – is at the top of almost every list, ahead of Willie Mays, Hank Aaron, Ted Williams, and all the other ballplayers before and since. He was the GOAT (the Greatest of All Time.)

The Babe was bigger than life in every way. He not only played big, he lived big – drank heavily, reportedly went to brothels and partied, bought fancy cars, and occasionally came to the ballpark with a hangover. Most overlooked his indiscretions, as he was also likeable, flamboyant, and he loved kids – and he delivered results on the diamond. He was a star. And Ruth helped save the national pastime. With MLB's legitimacy in doubt following the 1919 World Series, where the White Sox threw it for the Reds for $100,000 from gamblers (there's that trust issue again), the Babe slugged 54 homers in 1920 and then 59 in 1921. He, rather than the "Black Sox," became the story.

As his remarkable career began winding down, Babe met with Ed Barrows, general manager for the Yankees. Babe explained that he wanted to manage the Yankees when he retired, and given his performance on the field, he believed he had earned the right to do so. Barrows responded, "Babe, you can't manage yourself. How are you going to manage other men?" So, the great Babe Ruth never did manage the Yankees, nor any other team.

On paper – record-breaking stats year after year – one might think Babe Ruth could be a great team manager. So often, organizations promote those who are outstanding "doers" in their respective jobs. If they perform well at doing, it is assumed, or hoped, they will perform well further up the ladder. Or perhaps it is often thought they earned the opportunity to lead.

But leadership requires largely different qualities than being a great doer. No major league baseball owner believed the Babe, the greatest baseball player of all time, had those qualities essential to lead others, and so no owner put their trust in him to lead a team.

Professor Harry Kraemer of Northwestern University's Kellogg School of Management said, "If I don't know myself, how can I lead myself. And if I cannot lead myself, how can I lead others."[3] This was exactly the point Ed Barrows made to the Babe about coaching the Yankees. A leader must be able to manage themselves. Dee Hock, who founded Visa, said, "If you want to lead others, spend fifty percent of your time on yourself."

Self-leadership is a key to successful leadership, and this is particularly important in the context of change. At the end of the day, a person who cannot lead themselves loses the trust of others. A person who cannot lead themselves is prone to say one thing but do another. That is, they might talk the talk, but cannot walk the walk. They may say, using the Babe as an example, don't drink the night before a ballgame. But he did on occasion.

A person capable of self-leadership is not prone to irrational outburst. Those who aren't so capable will have such outbursts, and trust is destroyed. Many of us have worked for a mercurial boss at one point or another. It's miserable. Their explosions are both irrational and unpredictable. You cannot trust a mercurial boss to treat you reasonably or fairly, much less to make sound decisions.

Some years before joining Bridgestone Americas, I was practicing law at a law firm. I was working with a more senior lawyer on a case, and he called me while I was traveling on business. He proceeded to scold me because another lawyer made a significant mistake in a legal memo she had written. He claimed that it was my responsibility to know that this other lawyer was doing work on the case in my absence and to oversee that lawyer's work. The thing was, I had not assigned the memo to that other lawyer. Rather, the senior lawyer went around me, which was his prerogative, and assigned it in my absence while I was traveling. Yet, I was scolded because that other lawyer made a mistake.

This was consistent with the senior lawyer's reputation for being exceedingly difficult to work with and mercurial. Whatever

---

[3] Teneshia Jackson Warner, "How to Become a Values-Based Leader," *Success*, October 28, 2013.

trust that had been created between the two of us was gone. I could not possibly trust that lawyer to be reasonable and, when push came to shove, to have my back.

Aristotle put it so eloquently: "Anybody can become angry – that is easy. But to be angry with the right person and to the right degree and at the right time and for the right purpose, and in the right way – that is not within everybody's power and is not easy."[4] But as difficult as it might be, that is part of building trust, and that is essential for a leader to get people to follow him on the change journey.

The lack of emotional control has additional disastrous consequences both to change and, more generally, to leadership. People around the leader will minimize their interaction with him or her, only report the good news, and offer little in the way of new ideas as any idea can provoke an eruption. The change effort and the leader lose the enormous benefit of true discussion and debate in search of the best change strategies and tactics. It also hurts productivity and zaps the energy out of a department, unit, or entire company. One bad apple can spoil the whole bunch.

To manage one's anger requires insight, self-control, and discipline. When a leader can do that, that person has gone a long way toward building trust. This begins with the acknowledgment that emotions are not good or bad. Rather, it is how we respond to our emotions that can be labeled effective or ineffective. The response is the behavior, what is seen by others. The emotion is what is felt. When a person can separate the two, take a step back and identify what they are feeling, they then can better choose how they will respond.

This does not mean that any display of emotions is entirely taboo. Certainly, positive emotions, excitement, enthusiasm, are

---

[4]Neca C. Smith, "Anger Management at Work – Aristotle's Way," *Corporate Wellness Magazine*, https://www.corporatewellnessmagazine.com/article/anger-management-at.

important and can be wonderfully contagious. Negative, albeit measured, emotions can be used to great effect, but sparingly.

On one occasion, I intentionally decided to admonish a teammate in a staff meeting. But my primary reason for doing so was to ensure that others would never make the kind of mistake that he made.

In a staff meeting, a middle level executive reported that we had missed an opportunity to improve our sales of agricultural tires in a South American country. He said the market was taking off and we weren't fully participating. I asked why we missed the opportunity, and the executive, who clearly had not thought through the logical flow of the discussion, said he was waiting for management to give direction on whether to produce more of those tires. I pressed him, and the executive conceded that he had never raised the issue with his boss, or anyone else for that matter. I then had no choice. I did not yell, but I forcefully made it clear to him, and implicitly to everyone else in the room, that it was his job to either make the decision or at minimum bring the issue to his manager for a decision, neither of which he had done.

My message: people were to act (here again, a propensity for action) or at a minimum they were to raise issues when they were unsure how to proceed or needed the involvement of others beyond their sphere of influence. Silence and sitting on one's hands were not viable options in this organization.

There is much to leading oneself. The starting point is an understanding of your own interests, values, strengths, and weaknesses. You must be willing to peel back the layers of your personality, do the hard work necessary to grow, learn, understand, and at least acknowledge your weaknesses, insecurities, ego, and emotions. This is self-awareness.

A self-aware leader better understands how to respond to different emotions. They have the ability to first recognize the emotion they are feeling, then make choices on how to behave. They do not let the emotion control them; they control the emotion. This is half of the many lessons of emotional intelligence: knowing and managing oneself. When this is accomplished, that is leading oneself. It is then that a person is able to lead others.

Leaders have choices as to how they behave. When they master the appropriate behavior for the situation, relationships flourish, trust increases, and commitment to the changes the leader is seeking to make is strengthened.

4. Humility and Empathy as an Element of Trust

There are different definitions of humility. One dictionary defines it as "the state or quality of being lowly in mind; modesty; meekness."[5] It is hard to imagine a successful leader who is meek. The definition I use for humility does not go so far as to be meek or timid. Rather, the way I use humility is closer to the way it is defined by Merriam-Webster: "freedom from pride or arrogance."

Pride, if it is not excessive, can be a good thing. Pride in one's work drives better quality as does pride in the outcomes of one's work. Excessive pride, however, closes one's mind from listening to others, from recognizing one's own mistakes and thus learning from experience, and from unbiased feedback. Excessive pride stunts growth. All the world is about balance, and this applies with full force to pride.

In this context, I propose a definition of humility that is more consistent with the concept of "freedom from . . . arrogance." As one of my mentors put it, "Sooner or later, arrogance will kill you." He was speaking figuratively, of course, but, in some circumstances, it can be as literal as an intoxicated person who believes they can still drive safely. As Albert Einstein said, "The only thing more dangerous than ignorance is arrogance."[6]

---

[5] *The Winston Dictionary*, College Edition.
[6] CoolNSmart.com, "Arrogance Quotes, Sayings about Arrogant People," https://www.coolnsmart.com/arrogance_quotes/.

Steve Jobs, by all accounts, did not lack confidence. But he also certainly did not believe that he had all the answers. One of his key formulas for success was to hire the smartest people he could find. Once hired, he didn't tell them how to do their job. To the contrary, as noted earlier, he hired them "so they can tell us what to do."[7]

Good ideas can come from anywhere. Similarly, I have yet to come across anyone who had a monopoly on good ideas. To be sure, I came across people who believed they did, but this was arrogance more than brilliance. Humility enables two incredibly important, albeit basic, dynamics in driving change, indeed, in the context of all leadership.

First, it opens a leader up to the ideas of others. A humble leader knows what she doesn't know. She does not have all the right answers, and she is not afraid to admit that truth. Business is complex. Being open to the ideas of others is critical in all circumstances, but especially when driving massive change. After all, the precise changes to be made and how to make them go a long way to the success of the change effort. The discussion and debate that occurs in search of the best answers often results in a better solution than the leader could have come up with on their own.

George Washington held his war councils with his top generals to determine the best strategies and tactics to confront the superior British forces. Upon becoming president, he filled his cabinet with the likes of the brilliant Thomas Jefferson and Alexander Hamilton. Abraham Lincoln placed some of his greatest political rivals in the cabinet, men who certainly weren't wallflowers. Dwight D. Eisenhower, Supreme Allied Commander in WWII and then president of the United States (not a bad career by any standard), famously said, "The greatest

---

[7] Victor Lipman, "The Best Sentence I Ever Read about Managing Talent," *Forbes*, September 25, 2018.

leaders are the ones smart enough to hire people smarter than them."

The second dynamic of humility, and not to be understated, is having participated in the formulation of the idea and recognizing its likely viability, other members of the team are better positioned to embrace the idea, take ownership of it, and help sell and drive it through the ranks. The chances of the idea successfully being implemented are then greatly enhanced. It is not the leader's success; it is the team's success.

A humble leader doesn't make it about the leader; rather, they make everything about the organization and its people. The great Paul "Bear" Bryant, one of the most successful college football coaches ever, famously said, "If anything goes bad, I did it. If anything goes semi-good, we did it. If anything goes really good, then you did it. That's all it takes to get people to win football games for you."

A lot, indeed, comes from the simple quality of humility.

Another aspect of building trust is empathy. Similar to humility, it allows a leader to recognize the emotions others experience. This understanding helps leaders manage their relationships. The unknown, the uncertainty of the future and how it will impact them, often drives many to resist change. A leader with empathy is better able to connect with those who need to help make change happen. Conversely, a leader who lacks empathy or simply doesn't give a damn about the trials and tribulations of those he or she leads is unlikely to build the bond of trust that is so important in driving change.

We know this to be true from our life experiences. If a person has no interest in your issues, your plight, you tend to avoid that person. Conversely, a person who shows interest and acknowledges what you might be going through is the kind of person in whom you will confide, and then, importantly, listen to. (This also is the value of listening before seeking to be listened to.) There is a bond, a sense of security and safety with such a person. In a word, trust.

The imprimatur of empathy is the way change is implemented. Many policy changes can have profound effects on people, their livelihood, their level of motivation and loyalty, how they treat customers and colleagues, and certainly whether they will go the extra mile in getting work done. Empathy enables a change leader to implement policies in a way that is motivating, or at least, not nearly as de-motivating, as they might be otherwise.

During my tenure as CEO, we learned that we needed to change an aspect of our compensation strategy. We discovered that for certain parts of the organization our compensation was substantially above market while certain other parts of the organization were not sufficiently competitive. This was both a cost issue, a recruiting issue, and a retention issue. It had to be dealt with. The question was how.

It is hard to imagine a more de-motivating announcement than to hear you have been overpaid and your compensation is being reduced. The Executive Committee grappled with this for several meetings, reviewing the data, trying to decide how to fix it, and determine the timeline for implementation. Ultimately, the committee concluded that new compensation programs needed to be phased in over several years, relying in significant part on making fixes as people retired or were promoted over time, gradually bringing the company's compensation program into line with where, strategically, we believed it needed to be.

We explained the problem and rolled out the program during town hall meetings across the organization so we could answer questions as best as possible and also to let people vent. We didn't hide behind a memo or a video. The announcement of the new program largely became a non-event, as the changes were phased in such a way that was sensitive, empathetic if you will, to the needs and emotions of the people impacted. The phased-in changes over several years were much easier to swallow than an abrupt and de-motivating announcement. Empathy is what drove our final conclusions. And that, in turn, helps build trust that we would truly consider the impact of our actions.

5. Walking the Walk as an Element of Trust

Words are just words unless they are backed up with actions. A leader must talk the talk and walk the walk. If a leader says one thing but does another, that builds cynicism, not trust. Actions speak louder than words.

If, for example, a leader wants courage and candor from others, the leader must, in both words and actions, create an environment that welcomes it. This is done by setting a tone and responding to questions, ideas, and debate in such a way so that others feel safe putting their thoughts on the table.

In Chapter 7, I discuss the importance of culture and how to change it. A necessary part of changing the culture was that I had to live that new culture. I, of course, could not possibly expect others to change their behaviors to fit the new cultural blueprint if I did not fully and completely embrace that blueprint in both my words and behaviors.

Imagine a leader who says she welcomed debate and discussion, but if someone mustered the courage to speak up, that leader then shot them down or dismissed the idea with an off-the-cuff comment. The discussion would stop there and so would the inclination of others to share their thoughts. Such a leader might say she welcomes debate, but others would know she didn't mean it.

But walking the walk – or leading by example – is not the be all, end all of change or even leadership. Rather, it is one important aspect of it. So often, I have heard people say that their leadership style is to lead by example. Setting the right example is very important to be sure, and it is certainly a key element in creating trust. That is walking the walk.

But successful leaders know that there is much more to leading others than setting the right example. A leader must set high expectations for the performance and results of the team and hold others to those expectations. A leader must give feedback – both positive and constructive – and that requires honesty and has little to do, at least directly, with "leading by example." And, if a leader truly walks the walk, he too should be open to receiving feedback.

Further, a leader must make sure he or she has the right team (Chapter 8) and that the team is well-aligned and focused on execution (discussed in Chapters 9 and 10, respectively). A leader must know when to promote and when to jettison team members and be willing to act on it. A leader must know when and how to delegate what and to whom so that the task at hand is likely to succeed without micromanagement, thus causing the leader to devote his or her attention away from those things that are better suited to his or her role. A leader must decide what changes are needed in the organization and its strategy, and then drive those changes. These and so many other important actions are essential to successful leadership, but they have little to do with leading by example.

Walking the walk is, therefore, one of the core tenets of both driving change and successful leadership. It is an essential component of trust. But effective leadership does not stop with leading by example; it is doing all the other things a leader must do.

Propensity for Action

As mentioned previously, in the early 1990s the company had organized itself into many different divisions to assist with the integration of the Bridgestone and Firestone operations and to drive operational improvement. The strategy worked.

Over time many of these divisions developed their own purchasing, IT, human resources, legal, marketing and many other support functions, and those functions operated largely autonomously from one another. This allowed for each such operation to proceed as it deemed best for its ultimate success. The trade-off was increased cost structure in having redundant support functions addressing many of the same issues.

In 2008, the then head of Bridgestone Americas' IT team suggested that the company adopt a shared services model. A shared service model is where various support groups such as IT, human resources, purchasing, etc., are centralized but support each of the various operational divisions. The goal is to ultimately reduce the costs by avoiding redundancy and driving consistency throughout the operations. Such a model, he argued, would allow Bridgestone Americas to leverage its purchasing power and reduce its overhead costs. Overhead is, as one might understand, a frequent source of discussion in mature industries.

For roughly two years, the topic would occasionally come up for discussion, but senior management was reluctant to pull the trigger on a shared service model for fear of interfering with the operations of our various divisions. Such a huge step would have been traumatic for the organization and was not to be undertaken lightly or impulsively.

But some of us were strongly of the view this was the right thing for the organization. And so, as discussed more fully below, shortly after I became the CEO, we proceeded to make that change.

The bottom line is this: it is a leader's responsibility to drive change. A leader must have a propensity for action. This term was chosen rather than the word "action" alone as it implies the appropriate level of care, thought, and debate prior to taking significant action. A leader must, usually through discussion and debate with others, fully consider the consequences of major changes that are to occur. As mentioned above, that collaborative process also helps others embrace the decisions. But then, the leader must have the decisiveness and courage to move forward. Just like Washington, action must be a change leader's inclination. That is a propensity for action.

A leader must then, directly or through others, put change into action. Leadership must insist on change and a leader either must drive that change directly or, at a minimum, hold others responsible and accountable for driving it. Without a propensity for action, change will simply not happen.

* * *

I have often heard of change efforts that failed because the leader who must drive the change doesn't. The leader, in effect, abdicates responsibility. They leave it to others without holding them accountable to make change happen, without being sufficiently directly involved and providing the support needed to make change stick. At the end of the day, the leader must drive change. Indeed, this is arguably a leader's greatest responsibility.

Does that mean that the change ideas must originate with the leader? Of course not. Many of the changes made at Bridgestone Americas were suggested by others, both inside and outside the company. But if those changes are to become a reality, they must first be fully embraced by the leader, and then driven appropriately by the leader (directly or indirectly by holding others' feet to the fire). Otherwise, the changes simply will not happen.

To a certain degree change can be delegated. Indeed, there almost certainly will be significant delegation and reliance on others to help move the cause forward. But a leader cannot hope that others will make the changes that need to occur without some degree of meaningful participation, support, and oversight by the leader. Indeed, it is the leader who must "sell" the changes, that is part and parcel of an effective vision, discussed more fully in the following chapter. Then the leader must, as discussed later, both ensure alignment throughout the team and have a never yielding resolve, that is, focused execution, to see the changes through.

The head of a department or division can make changes in their operations without the direct involvement of the CEO. But a team within that department cannot make broader changes to the department without the support and leadership of the department head. However, a department head's sphere of influence stops there. She cannot make changes to the broader organization without the CEO's direct and unyielding support. This is axiomatic.

The specific changes a leader seeks to make are very important. Are they the right ones in terms of culture, strategy, business efficiency and effectiveness? Is this where the business has been or where the business needs to go? As they say in hockey, skate to where the puck is going, not to where it is. Having the right team (people) at the table to ensure that the decisions are the best ones under the circumstances is critical.

But at least as important is whether the leader is sufficiently determined and involved in making those changes become a reality. That is critical for success. So often, a leader either sees a problem and can't effectively address it, the leader is blind to the problem to begin with, or the leader does not have the courage to tackle the problem. The job of change leaders is to see what the future can or should be and make the appropriate changes, because no one else can possibly do it. Successful leaders, armed with their propensity for action, take and demand thoughtful action, and they will not accept stagnation.

* * *

I was told months in advance that I would become the CEO. During that time, before the announcement, I met with the person who was to be the COO several times a week, either at night at one another's house or over the weekends, to discuss the company – people, governance structure, culture, strategy, operations, and ways we might take the company to the next level. We brought in two consultants to work with us. Together, our work resulted in a blueprint for the future state of the company, which was shared with the global CEO of Bridgestone.

We recognized that not all the changes could be made immediately as the organization could only accept so much at one time. Over time, we made changes to the blueprint as we saw necessary, and we discussed it with our team in the fullness of time. Those discussions inevitably resulted in some changes and tweaks. But the bottom line was we carefully discussed many of the changes that needed to be made and we didn't shy away from taking action.

Immediately upon taking over the helm of Bridgestone Americas, we decided it was time to part ways with a senior business executive in the company. While talented and well-liked, we did not think he was a cultural fit for the organization we wanted to create. Such action – letting go a senior executive – was rare in our organization. The announcement that he was leaving the organization sent reverberations throughout the company. It was a new day.

That decision was followed up by announcing sweeping governance changes. Most successful companies have strong governance models that help ensure effective decision-making, transparency, debate, and accountability. Governance is to an organization what a foundation is to a building. The entirety of the organization rests upon its governance structure. A company that lacks strong governance is at significant risk, and in all likelihood, it is destined for trouble.

Governance changes may not sound earth shattering to some, but it was significant for our company. In fact, one of the higher-ranking executives urged that we stay away from using the term "governance" in describing the changes as he believed the organization would react negatively to it. Many would view the change as creating a bureaucracy, he argued, which could slow down operations, increase costs, and ultimately increase workloads.

Although his recommendation was well-intended, I declined to follow it. That simply wasn't my style. It wasn't authentic. It wasn't honest. You can call a horse a cow, but it's still a horse. The company would, in my opinion, see right through the wordsmithing and my credibility, which I guarded zealously, would be needlessly brought into question. I would lose the trust I was trying to build.

To keep to the promise of honesty and transparency, I explained that a strong governance structure improves the decision-making process, drives improved coordination among different parts of an organization, and helps ensure greater involvement in the company's direction among the entire management team. Process, when taken seriously, does matter. Good governance is a strength, not a weakness. Many of the best run companies in the world have strong and vibrant governance structures. Our governance, while good, could be better, copying those of other great companies.

First, we announced that we were adding several Japanese executives who worked and lived in Japan to Bridgestone Americas' Board of Directors. Previously, the Bridgestone Americas Board did not have any Japanese members. Another senior Japanese executive who worked in the United States was appointed chairman of the board.[8] It made all the sense in the world that the parent company would have seats on the board of its largest subsidiary.

This, along with the management change discussed previously, stunned the organization. Some people thought including Japan to that extent might hinder our ability to act quickly. But I saw it differently. It would enhance our ability to act together and symbiotically with the parent company. Our obligation, our job, was to work with our parent company to the greatest extent possible.

For the new Japanese directors to meaningfully participate in important business decisions, it would require that the options and rationale for any given course of action be fully explained to them, just like they would be to outside directors in a publicly traded company. These "outside" board members also would help ensure transparency, communication, and coordination with the parent company half a world away.

---

[8] Even though the chairman and CEO positions were separated, it was made explicit to me that my boss was the global CEO in Tokyo. Toward the end of my career with Bridgestone, I also was the chairman of Bridgestone Americas in addition to my responsibilities as CEO and president.

In any event, I had no interest in a rubber stamp board. Rather, I wanted a board that provided independent review and oversight and that brought fresh ideas to the table. The organization and ultimately the shareholders would be the beneficiaries of such a process.

But that was just the beginning of implementing stronger governance standards. The second step was the creation of an Executive Committee, which messaged that Bridgestone Americas' senior team would have an even greater role than it had before in determining the fate of the organization. From that point forward, the senior most people in the company would have a direct role in helping to decide and shape the company's future, and that role extended well beyond their specific job functions.

The first work in the Executive Committee, though, was to create a culture for the committee itself. The key tenets of that culture required each member to be candid and be present, meaning each had to pay attention and commit to no cell phone or laptop use or other work during committee meetings. Each member was to "wear their enterprise hat" as opposed to their function or team hat. In other words, they were to opine and advocate on behalf of the entire company, not their respective parts of the business.

Each member of the committee was expected to listen actively to others, be innovative, and stay strategic. And, finally, Executive Committee members were to speak with one voice when meetings were over; in other words, passive aggressive behavior would not be tolerated.

Creating this culture within the Executive Committee was neither easy nor immediate. The committee was new to every member, and we all had to learn and create the culture together.

I had to demonstrate to Executive Committee members that I was not just asking them to rubber stamp my decisions or the decisions of the COO. Their voices were meaningful and influential and would always be seriously considered if not followed. That took considerable time and effort. As issues were discussed, I made a point to be the last to state my views, first taking in the counsel of other members of the Executive Committee. Over time, the team began to trust me, to believe that I truly respected their views, and disagreements with me were appreciated (as long as it was not taken outside the committee room; that is, we had to always speak with one voice outside of the committee room).

Further, I often had to keep discussions on point. Someone might, for example, raise an issue or make a proposal. There is a natural tendency among others to want to make their points before the first person's point is fully addressed. I often had to keep the discussion focused on the first point before moving the discussion to the issues that another person wanted to make. It sounds minor, but it was critical for everyone to feel like they had truly been heard.

We needed the Executive Committee's help to drive our agenda throughout the organization. Committee members could reach out into the depths of the organization in ways neither the CEO nor the COO could. The downside, of course, was that their buy-in was critical, and that often is more time consuming than top-down decision-making. But such is life for those driving change. Indeed, as President Eisenhower said, leadership is getting people to do what you want, and they don't know you want them to do it. That takes both time and effort.

Not surprisingly, the results of the Executive Committee discussions improved the various programs and strategies before the committee, and it helped improve communication among different parts of the organization. The time involved in the Executive Committee was well worth the effort.

A third governance change was to create a board-level compensation committee, consisting of, among others, key human resource executives within the company and key executives from Japan. This committee would ultimately be responsible for setting (subject to final approval of the Executive

Committee and the board) all significant compensation programs for the organization. This ensured both buy-in and vetting and it eliminated any opportunity for self-dealing.[9] Virtually every Fortune 500 company has such a committee, and now we did as well.

Another governance change was the creation of a Risk and Governance Committee and a Product, Development and Research Committee. The former would serve as an independent body to evaluate and advise the board on the major risks facing the company and to evaluate if the company was sufficiently managing its risk profile. The latter was to help ensure that Bridgestone Americas' R&D focus was both consistent with its business strategy and that products were performing well in the marketplace in the minds of the end-user. The latter point was, of course, critical for our company's continued success. It also would help ensure that the key performance characteristics of our tires were meeting, if not exceeding, the wants and needs of the end-user of those tires – who, as described in Chapter 7, came to be known as "The Boss."

At least initially, and not surprisingly, some did complain bitterly that this expansive governance structure created an unnecessary bureaucracy. That it slowed down some decisions was a certainty.

But the new governance processes forced executives to better think through proposals. It also helped improve communication among top executives across the various operations. They started to talk with each other to a greater extent than ever before, and in the process, they were building relationships with one another. The Executive Committee was deeply involved in the major decisions facing the organization, and as a result, better decisions were made than would have been made without its input. Taking these new responsibilities

---

[9] We did not, to the best of my knowledge, have any issues of self-dealing. Nonetheless, this check and balance is good governance that is widely adopted by most large organizations.

seriously forced everyone to make better, more informed, and coordinated decisions. The ultimate beneficiaries were our shareholders.

Because the COO and I both sat on all but the risk committee, the new governance structure also created additional opportunities for us to interact more regularly with many different executives across the company. In so doing, we not only learned what they and their staffs were thinking, but we had the chance to create and reinforce a culture where we listened and invited debate; a culture that welcomed new ideas; a culture that forced deep dives into the data before critical decisions were made.

This example also gave other executives a model to emulate as they worked through issues with their respective teams in different parts of the company.

In addition to the governance changes, we restructured much of the business. Historically, each of the heads of consumer tire sales, the retail tire and automotive service team, truck tire sales, agricultural tire sales, off-road tire sales, the Latin American (which included Mexico, Central America, and South America) tire business, manufacturing, R&D, and the diversified business as well as each of the function teams reportedly directly to the CEO. Given how large Bridgestone Americas was, that was too much.

We created the position of President of the Consumer Tire Business, that is, tires for passenger cars. Rather than the company-owned retail stores and wholesale tire business acting independently of one another, they would report to the same person, who would be responsible to ensure that the two coordinated their strategies and other activities. That person then reported to the COO.

A similar change was made in the North American commercial tire business so that the truck tire wholesale and retail operations, as well as the off-road tire and agricultural tire businesses, could coordinate on costs, strategies, and the like. That person also reported directly to the COO. This had the added benefits of pushing accountability down the leadership hierarchy.

Over the next few years, nearly all of Bridgestone's subsidiaries – from Europe to Asia – adopted much of this governance structure.

Some questioned the governance actions and restructuring on their merits, and some were disappointed they were not selected to lead one of those two major business units. Apart from the fact that the accumulated results bore out the wisdom of these decisions, I strongly believed this to be the right governance and organizational structure for the company. Most importantly for our purposes here, we did not shy away from taking the action we thought was needed to succeed, and we did so promptly upon assuming our responsibilities.

It took a propensity for action. That was our job if we were going to take the company to the next level. Make things happen. Carefully, thoughtfully, compassionately, but decisively.

* * *

These governance changes were just the beginning. Throughout the rest of this book, I discuss many of the changes we made strategically, culturally, and from a people perspective. Each of those changes required a propensity for action. But as a prelude to those sweeping changes, we needed to make the case for why the change was needed, which was a difficult task in itself.

Change can be thrust upon an organization through necessity, such as when facing bankruptcy or a pandemic. In such instances, the need for change, and with it the vision, can be readily understood and accepted and is, in that sense, more reactive than proactive.

In other situations, the need for change is less clear, and the case for both it and the vision must be persuasive. That was the case for Bridgestone Americas because many in the company saw no need for change. Most years we received very good bonuses. Management reinforced this message by saying our performance was great and that we had the best team in the industry. Understandably, the organization loved the bonus money and the messages.

Against this backdrop, we had to make the case for change if teammates were to buy into the changes.

To start the process, I called an offsite meeting with the top 30 or so executives in the company shortly after assuming my new responsibilities. At the meeting a series of slides prepared by the finance team was presented showing the state of the company's financial affairs. We explained that our ratio of profits to revenues had room for improvement based on top performers in the industry, and our shareholders expected more of us.

Some argued that the US tire market was far more competitive than other markets around the world. They said that because the market in the United States was more competitive, higher profit margins just weren't as realistic.

We continued to paint our financial picture. Including legitimate, but off-balance-sheet financing as well as all our pension obligations, our debt load was more significant than we wanted. That coupled with our cash flow made it more difficult than we wanted to invest in our future.

Our profits had been slowly recovering from the Ford-Firestone recall, but then we were hit hard by the 2008–2009 Great Recession, as were all tire companies, essentially wiping out the gains we had made.

Then we reviewed the rolling five-year commitments we had made to the parent company in which we projected our long-term results. We compared those to our actual results. Perennially, our results fell short of the long-term projections we had promised. This naturally disappointed our parent company and Bridgestone shareholders globally, and it hurt our credibility.

We closed by explaining that our parent company and Bridgestone shareholders globally were demanding more from our operations, even more than we had delivered when times were at our best. Going forward, we explained that we had to do even better than we had when results were at their strongest.

Our message was not directed at any one person or one group, but at all of us as a team. The point had been made. Things had to improve. Whatever we had been doing wasn't enough.

We closed by explaining that we didn't have all the answers and we invited their ideas. We did make it clear, however, that the status quo had to change. We ended the meeting so this team of executives could reflect on what they had learned and process their emotions.

Explaining these facts to a team of senior executives was one thing. They spoke the language of finance and were used to seeing and could understand complex financial charts. The next challenge was getting the broader employee base to recognize and accept the need for change.

We decided to hold a series of town hall meetings throughout the major offices of the organization. When I assumed the role of CEO, the concept of town hall meetings with the CEO was new for our company. We knew however that we had to explain the current state of the company's affairs, and we had to answer questions that employees were sure to have. If things were going to change, we needed to create a case for change that our employees could understand. We prepared a slide deck that would be readily understandable to all, including those who weren't used to reading financial statements. Most importantly, we began the town hall meetings with a hypothetical business example.

Imagine, I said at the beginning of the meetings, that you own an ice cream shop. That ice cream store represents your livelihood. Here was the question: Let's say you sell $100,000 worth of ice cream in one year. How much would you expect to have in profits at the end of the year? The answers were all over the board, but most ranged from $50,000 to $80,000.

I then showed a chart explaining that on average over the last several years the company made a much smaller percent of profits than anyone in the room would have expected. This was eye-opening for the group. In the ice cream shop example, the owner would have not been satisfied with the profit picture.

The company's total debt and cash flow were then explained in terms everyone could understand. Our transparency was not only enlightening, but also helped build trust.

Finally, I explained that our parent company and global shareholders expected more from us and that we needed to take the organization to the next level. No one argued with us. They couldn't. The seeds of change had been planted. But, again, it is one thing for people to recognize the intellectual need for change, it is a wholly different thing for them to emotionally accept change and to embrace the hard work necessary to make it happen.

We didn't discuss the changes that needed to be made, and indeed, we still didn't know the full scope of all the changes that would have to occur. Nor were we prepared to limit ourselves by listing the changes at that time and then coming back later and saying, "Oh, by the way, there's more that needs to change." We wanted the organization to process what they had learned. The status quo was about to be a thing of the past. This was a big paradigm shift that needed time to sink in.

Having tilled the soil, if you will, shortly thereafter we announced a company-wide cost reduction effort, called "Bridge to Excellence." Under this program, with the help of an outside consultant, many significant operational processes were to be reviewed with the goal of improving the efficiencies of the processes. This was something that had not been done in at least 20 years, and perhaps much longer than that. The expectation was that some processes would be eliminated altogether, and others significantly improved.

This, in turn, led to the creation and implementation of a shared service model for the organization. As discussed earlier, each business unit traditionally had its own HR, legal, marketing, IT, and PR teams. As part of our effort, we centralized these functions so we could improve our efficiencies and cost structure, and so we had consistent processes and policies across the Americas. Under the new structure, the head of each function would be ultimately responsible to ensure that the right hand and left hand worked together, and that their respective functions fully satisfied the needs of each business unit. For example, the IT systems adopted by one business unit had to be consistent with the IT infrastructure for the entire organization.

But improving efficiency also meant right sizing the organization, and Bridgestone Americas was thrown into a tizzy. Eliminating jobs and reducing the workforce was something that had not been experienced at Bridgestone Americas, at least during my tenure with the company. Understandably, people were scared, and so the subsequent resistance to the efficiency improvements was both overt and subvert.

The right-sizing effort was a massive undertaking. One of our best and brightest executives was appointed to lead this effort, with the goal to reduce administrative costs by 20 percent. He did an outstanding job. He was honest with all, open with the agenda, knew when to update us and when to get us involved to overcome resistance, insistent in making the needed progress, and all the while gentle in his style.

In meeting after meeting, department and team heads fought and pleaded that their teams be opted-out of the program. We could not and did not give in. We persisted in demanding that each part of the organization reduce its cost structure by 20 percent, and, ultimately, that is what happened.

Overseeing a reduction effort usually doesn't create fans. This executive was at risk of being stigmatized with the reputation of being the corporate butcher. We knew that would not serve his career well in the long run. Further, it was clear that he was destined for bigger and better things. So, when the Bridge to Excellence project was completed, he was assigned to run the truck tire division in the Western part of the United States, both to round out his experience in that part of the business and to give the organization time to disconnect him from all his extraordinary, yet often unpleasant, efforts. Two years later, he deservingly became the CFO for Bridgestone Americas and, when I retired, he was promoted to COO.

More broadly though, the necessary cost-cutting efforts damaged the organization's morale. Teammates were scared and angry. Friends and colleagues were let go. The pain was real. In time the organization, the social system made up of people, began to heal. They saw how the process improvements often made their work better and they began to see the possibilities of working smarter, not harder, and that the improved efficiencies produced better financial results. Importantly, the strong financial results reinforced that the changes were needed, which in turn helped result in strong bonuses even though the bonus plans were based on aggressive targets. Equally important, the organization clearly got the message: change was the order of the day.

The bottom line is this, however: change takes leadership, and that means having a propensity for action.

* * *

Cost control is, in most industries, essential. That said, unless a company's strategy is to compete largely on price, which certainly wasn't Bridgestone Americas' strategy, a company cannot save its way to success. So, along with improving the company's cost structure, we pushed our tire operations to take the bold step of raising prices several times over a two-year period. This was done just as the country and the world were coming out of the Great Recession.

At that time, someone could buy a set of four tires for $100, and one's life and well-being could depend on how those tires performed. Yet, in 2010 that same person might pay considerably more for a pair of name-brand basketball shoes (a testament to the power of marketing).

Price increases in the tire business were relatively rare because it is intensely competitive. But early on in my tenure raw material costs were rising significantly, and if Bridgestone Americas was going to fulfill its financial commitments to the parent company, it had to act.

Some executives were skeptical of the aggressive price hikes. But the risk was worth it. If the price increases didn't stick in the marketplace, at least we had tried; moreover, if they didn't stick, we would lose some short-term sales, but probably not much more than that. Fortunately, each of the price increases did stick as other manufacturers ultimately raised prices too, likely because they were struggling with the high raw material costs just as we were. And so, with these price increases our tires became considerably more profitable, particularly when raw material costs started dropping several months later.

This propensity for action also manifested itself in our tire production strategy. Our tire plants produced tires of all types and for a wide range of price points. Some tires were quite profitable, but the lower price point tires were not. This had to be fixed as well.

One option was to simply stop producing low-end tires. But this was problematic. Tire retailers and distributors needed these in their stores as an option for the price-conscious consumer. If our direct customers – that is, the independent tire dealer – could not get those low-cost tires from Bridgestone, they would get them from another source. And if that happened, those low-cost tire producers would likely seek to expand their sales into the more profitable segments in the future. That was a risk we were not prepared to take, so that option was off the table.

Instead, we decided to outsource production of low-end, off-brand tires (that is, tires other than Bridgestone and Firestone brands) to an off-shore manufacturer. To ensure sufficient quality of those low-price point tires, an expert from the quality assurance department evaluated the offshore manufacturer's capabilities. Satisfied with the report, production of these tires was shifted to that manufacturer. This stopped the bleeding of money on our production of low-end tires, and the company actually started to make a small profit on many of those out-sourced tires. Moreover, by eliminating low-end tires from Bridgestone's manufacturing plants, we immediately freed up manufacturing capacity for the more profitable high-end tires, and that also reduced the operational complexity in some of the plants.

Such changes continued on many fronts throughout the organization. All of this and so much more took persuasion, persistence, insistence and, above all, a propensity for action. In a word, leadership.

* * *

Change does not happen by a wish and a prayer, by talk and hope. Change leaders must have the courage to act, to drive changes, whether structural, strategic, and/or cultural. Of course, the changes must be wise, and that means thorough discussion, debate, scenario planning, and the like. At the end of the day, though, there must be a propensity for action. That is a hallmark of all successful change leaders.

Change creates uncertainty about the future. Will there be a place for me, and will I be able to survive in the new world? This uncertainty, this fear, drives resistance to change. One of the key ways a change leader eases these fears is by being trustworthy. Trust builds faith and hope that the leader's vision will work, will result in a better world, if you will. Trust also builds reason to believe that the leader will, at a minimum, treat others fairly, empathetically, and even compassionately.

Leaders build trust through their character, values, ethics, integrity, humility, empathy, and treatment of others. Effective leaders use language others understand. Corporate speak is a disease; it is vague at best and untrustworthy double-talk at worst. Trust also can be further strengthened through emotional control, that is self-leadership. Conversely, a lack of self-leadership will destroy trust.

A change leader must protect their credibility at all costs. Trust is the basis upon which people will follow a change leader. Then, a change leader must have a propensity for action. Trust and a propensity for action are two essential elements of change leadership. Armed with those critical assets, a change leader can boldly articulate and sell their vision for the new world.

6

Vision: Lesson #2

"If you don't know where you're going, you'll end up someplace else."
— *Yogi Berra*

ONE OF THE differences between a manager and a leader is Vision. A manager monitors activities that are current, making sure they are accomplished to standard and executed efficiently and effectively. A leader looks at what is and asks, "What can we become?" "Who do we want to be?" The answer to those questions is the *vision* for the future. And that vision is a critical requirement for any leader driving change.

Nelson Mandela had a vision for an integrated South Africa, and it did not include revenge against those who perpetuated apartheid. John F. Kennedy had a vision to send a man to the moon and return him safely to Earth. That culminated with Apollo 11 doing just that. Martin Luther King, Jr., had a vision of equality for African Americans. He immortalized his vision in his speech, "I Have a Dream," and while we are not there yet, we have made progress. Our Founding Fathers had a vision for a country not ruled by a monarch, but by a government "For the People, By the People, and Of the

People." The result was the United States, which, in turn, revolutionized governments around the world.

Vision is as important in the business and organizational realm as it is in the political realm. Steve Jobs had a vision to make computer technology accessible for everyone. Today, the iPhone or one its competitors (all of which are more powerful than the computers used to send a man to the moon) is nearly an appendage to roughly six billion people worldwide. Jeff Bezos started Amazon as an online bookstore, but his vision was for it to be an everything store. It certainly has become that. Less than 20 years ago, Elon Musk founded Tesla with a vision to drive the world's transition to electric vehicles. Today, by market capitalization, Tesla is by far the most valuable car company in the world, and many traditional car companies are starting to convert to electric cars.

As Alan Mullaly, CEO of the Ford Motor Company who saved the company during the Great Recession, stated, "It is the responsibility of a leader to articulate a clear and compelling vision for the organization." Indeed, this is certainly among a leader's greatest responsibilities.

A leader gives hope that the future will be brighter, greater, better than the present. As Napoleon put it, a leader is a dealer in hope. The vision, supported by a trustworthy leader who has the courage to act, provides that hope. Of course, if the leader is not trustworthy, then his vision will not be either. Thus, the importance of trust, discussed in the leadership chapter.

Vision does more. Don Groninger, Bridgestone Americas' general counsel who hired me into the company and who was the best boss I ever had, said "It's hard to get to your destination if you don't know where you're going." Vision gives direction in decision-making and actions. Our vision is what compelled us to make the many changes discussed throughout this book. If we were going to achieve our vision, we had to make the changes we have described in these pages. Further, vision is essential for alignment (Chapter 9). You need a vision to know what to align around.

A compelling vision creates enthusiasm and motivation for those within the team and it helps attract others to join the team. The importance of vision cannot be overstated and is certainly not to be taken lightly. Jeff Bezos put it well: "Be stubborn on vision; flexible on details."

* * *

Competition in the tire business is fierce. There were (and are) very capable, long-standing companies with excellent brands, technologies, and capabilities. Relatively new entrants were emerging from Asia with less expensive tires. There were very-low-cost tires coming into our markets from China and other Asian countries.

One advisor we talked with suggested that our vision should be no more than being a fast follower. But to me that could not be our vision for the company. I could not imagine telling the company we could only be second best. That advisor did not last long.

I saw it as my obligation to attempt to rebuild the greatness of the former Firestone Tire and Rubber Company, the forbearer of Bridgestone Americas. Such a vision also was consistent with the vision of the parent company, which rightfully had enormous pride in its products and history. Against this backdrop, the vision that emerged was straightforward and aggressive:

To Be an Outstanding Contributor to the Bridgestone Group and Be the Leader in Our Industries.

Many in the company might not have believed this vision was possible, but they certainly found it encouraging and refreshing. Those who had come from the Bridgestone side of the business shared the pride of our many tremendous technologies in such tires as the Blizzak snow and ice tire. Those who had come from the Firestone side of the business reveled in the glory of the past and longed for it to be recreated.

Visions must be sufficiently specific to help drive action and decisions. That is, the vision must be a description of what the organization, division, department, or team is to become and achieve. A vision is the desired future state.

To achieve our vision, we said we had to do four things, and do them very well. We named these things the Four Pillars (Figure 6.1), and they were sufficiently specific to give direction and alignment. Importantly, they became the foundation for every action and decision that needed to be made.

The first pillar was to be "Financially Successful." We had been significantly more focused on sales than profits. But both are important and so our future focus had to be on both.

One of our primary metrics for measuring financial performance was Return on Assets (ROA), which measures profits as a percent of assets. The global CEO made a commitment to Bridgestone shareholders to improve ROA to 6 percent for the entire organization. If our parent company was going to meet that commitment, Bridgestone Americas had to do significantly better. Additionally, our goal was to make the North American tire business sustainably profitable. We were not looking for a one-time quick profit that lasted for only a few years.

Figure 6.1   The Four Pillars

The second pillar was the "Brand Promise." Internally, the Bridgestone and Firestone brands meant something very special. They stood for quality, reliability, and excellence. That is indeed what the company always strived for.

For consumer tires – that is, tires for cars – we lost sight of what the consumer wanted and focused instead on what the car companies – our largest direct customers – wanted. Car companies often focused on tires that helped their car get great reviews by car critics and which also gave a great ride when people took the car on test drives. That was certainly understandable, and we were very good at making those customers (the car companies) happy. The end-user of our tires was pretty much considered to be our customers' customer. What we sometimes lost sight of was that the end-user wanted a tire that lasted a long time – 40,000 miles plus.

Historically, decisions were often made based on what car company customers wanted rather than on the spoken and unspoken needs and wants of the end-user. That had to change. If we were going to receive a premium price for our tires, consumers had to be thrilled with the performance of our products. That is, our products, all of them, had to meet or exceed the end-users' expectations. This also extended to our service operations. Great, reliable, honest products and service. That had to be Bridgestone Americas' Brand Promise.

The great comedian, George Carlin, said, "Most people work just hard enough not to get fired and get paid just enough money not to quit." An interesting perspective, to be sure. The third pillar focused on the people in the company, who we called teammates. While we had many outstanding performers, like most companies and organizations, there were also some people whose performance fell short. With a bold new vision, we also had to clarify and increase our performance expectations of our teammates. There were also skills and experiences we didn't have. Approaches to business management and technology had evolved, and we needed to evolve with it. This required us to bring in talent from the labor market, including some lateral talent at the executive level.

If we were to have any hope of achieving our vision, we needed to retain and attract teammates who shared this vision, and who had the business and cultural skills, and the drive, to help Bridgestone Americas achieve this vision. That is, we had to become a "Premier Place to Work" that attracted and retained the best talent.

This meant several things. People often perform up to the level that is tolerated. We had to change our level of what we "tolerated" to expect more of our people. Most could and did step up, we just had to expect it. Second, we had gaps, and we had to attract new people from the outside to fill those gaps. Finally, we had to become a dynamic, engaging place to work so we could both retain our highest performers and create enthusiasm within the organization. This is discussed at length in Chapters 7 and 8, on culture and people, respectively.

Finally, the fourth pillar focused on Bridgestone Americas' relationship with society. We pledged to be an "Outstanding Corporate Citizen." More specifically, we pledged to continue to be an outstanding corporate citizen.

Bridgestone Americas had been doing an excellent job of this. In fact, this was a source of enormous pride for the organization. We actively supported organizations that did great work in our communities, like the United Way. One of our tire plants achieved the near remarkable – the first tire plant in the United States if not the world to send zero waste to landfill. When a drought hit Tennessee farmers, our plant in Warren County helped negotiate favorable hay prices from out-of-state and then paid for the freight for hay to be shipped to area farmers. Our company-owned stores built and funded a facility located at an underprivileged high school to help students who weren't going to college learn a trade and get a good paying job as a certified auto mechanic. Pages upon pages could be filled with activities we did to help our communities, the underprivileged, children, and others in a time of need.

This needed to continue and even improve. We cared about the environment, the disadvantaged, those that fell on bad fortune from natural disasters, and the like. We strongly believed that business is not apart <u>from</u> society, but an important part <u>of</u> our society that can and should help make our lives better not just through well-paying jobs, but by being a community partner.

We also took safety in our factories and stores seriously. In fact, data indicated our safety record was second to none in the industry. I stubbornly held onto the belief that people have the right to go home from work in the same condition they arrived, except save being a little tired from putting in a good day at work.

But there was always room for improvement. We set a goal of zero workplace injuries. In all likelihood, this was unobtainable for a heavy manufacturing company. But striving for this goal would get us to a near perfect record, and by continually pushing ourselves, we made our workplace even safer. The leaders of our operations worked incredibly hard to make those continual safety improvements.

One executive we hired in 2011 to take over our roughly 2,200 consumer retail stores throughout the United States when the president of that business retired made safety one of his key focus points. He insisted that every meeting begin with a safety message. One year, on Halloween morning, one of his executives delivered the opening safety message at a staff meeting, and it was about being careful later that night when driving home from work because kids would be out trick-or-treating. So simple, so poignant, so caring. That is the kind of management most people would want to work for!

* * *

Sir Richard Branson, founder of Virgin Group, said, "If people aren't calling you crazy, you're not thinking big enough." Author and consultant Jim Collins advocates for setting big, hairy, audacious goals that everyone thinks are impossible to achieve. For us, the vision of being the leader in our industries and fulfilling the four pillars met Branson's and Collins's tests.

We were a good company, but Bridgestone Americas' market share and brand recognition in our major markets lagged some of our competitors. Some, perhaps many, thought I was out of touch with reality. How could we possibly overcome our competition in such a mature industry to truly be the leader in the tire industry?

How could we make major improvements in our financial results in the mature and highly competitive tire industry? Sure, we might do better than we had been, but the US tire market was ridiculously competitive, and our two major brands simply didn't have the prestige or pull of certain other brands, both in the United States and in Brazil, the largest market in South America. How could we possibly overcome those hurdles?

A premier place to work. Are you kidding? We are a tire company, which involves heavy manufacturing in a mature industry. We could never really be a premier place to work. We could never attract the cream of the crop. Never mind that Procter & Gamble, which makes diapers, toilet paper, and soap among other things, is an innovation and marketing juggernaut and reportedly a great company to work for.

That all had to change.

* * *

Creating a big, hairy, audacious vision isn't enough. The vision must appeal to the emotions of people throughout the organization. It should energize them, push them, give them something to be excited about and to work toward. That is exactly what President Kennedy did with his goal of sending a man to the moon and returning him safely to earth. That also is what Bill Gates did with his vision for a computer on every desk.

We tried to be bold with our vision for Bridgestone Americas. We saw an organization with two extraordinary brands, that could be vibrant, exciting, and empowering. We saw an organization that could be mentoring, growing, challenging, and on the cutting edge of our industries in how it goes to market.

One must go further still. As the famed General Electric CEO, Jack Welch, counseled, "Good business leaders create a vision, articulate the vision, passionately own the vision, and relentlessly drive it to completion." So, the vision must be repeated often and at every opportunity and enforced relentlessly. We consistently repeated and reinforced our vision in our town hall meetings.

The COO and I held semi-annual town hall meetings throughout the organization. Every meeting consisted of two parts. The first was a presentation about the state of the company. The second was questions and answers. For the update on the state of the company, every presentation had the same format. I began by repeating the company's vision and the Four Pillars, stating everything we do, every action we take, every project we work on must somehow advance one or more of the Four Pillars, or we probably should not be doing it. Then, we provided an update in the contexts of the Four Pillars.

Where did we stand on reaching our goal of being financially successful? This included a review of the company's financials, a discussion of various projects important to achieving those financial goals as well as hurdles we faced, and where we stood relative to our bonus payout goals.

Then we discussed what we were doing to fulfill the brand promise, the second pillar. This often included a discussion of new products and services to be launched that would help us fulfill the brand promise, as well as feedback we were receiving in the field about our products. We also discussed our marketing activities to get out the good word about our products and services. The next part of the update concerned what we were doing to become a premier place to work. This might include internal surveys on being a premier place to work, new HR programs, or the like.

We would then discuss important topics for us to be an Outstanding Corporate Citizen. Specifically, we reviewed our data on, and programs to improve, workplace safety, what we were doing to protect the environment and reduce our waste and carbon emissions, and other key civic or charitable activity in which the company was engaged.

Again and again, we hammered home the vision and the Four Pillars. Teammates soon began to expect an update on each of the Four Pillars during each town hall meeting. In turn, the Four Pillars and our vision helped drive change and action. We were, in Jack Welch's words, relentless in our pursuit of achieving our goals.

* * *

Bridgestone Americas was (and still is) the race tire supplier for IndyCar Racing, which includes the Indy 500. All cars use Firestone Racing Tires. In fact, one of our major competitors left the series in the mid-1990s after our tires began to dominate the winner's circle. Shortly after I became CEO, we became aware that our contract with IndyCar was up for renewal. Under the existing contract, sponsoring IndyCar through our tire supply agreement cost more money than we could afford. Yet, our extremely highly regarded race tires were a huge source of pride for our dealers and teammates. We made the very difficult decision that we had to significantly alter the terms as the tire supplier if we were going to continue with IndyCar Racing.

The negotiations failed to produce an agreement we could accept, so we issued a joint statement with IndyCar that we would be leaving the sport at the season's end. It was gut-wrenching as Firestone was synonymous with Indy racing ever since Ray Harroun won the first Indianapolis 500 race on Firestone tires in 1911. But we had to make the tough call to help achieve our vision. I received calls from dealers and even the legendary Mario Andretti urging that we reconsider. But if we shied away from the tough call, then the organization might have questioned whether we were truly committed to being financially successful. Put differently, to maintain our credibility, our trust, we had to be prepared to take Firestone out of IndyCar if that was what was needed to help achieve our vision.

By way of post-script, a few days after the announcement, the extraordinary happened. IndyCar team owners and drivers told IndyCar senior management that they would not race in the following season without Firestone tires. Why? Because the tires performed at the highest possible level and were remarkably reliable. IndyCar management then called me and asked if our last offer was still on the table. I said it was, of course, and within a week of our announcement that we were withdrawing from the sport, we announced that we had reached a new contract with IndyCar, and Firestone would be back for many years to come. This new contract was certainly helpful in us achieving the financial success that was so critical to our vision, and the unyielding pursuit of our vision was instrumental in achieving a new contract.

* * *

All decisions, actions, and efforts must seek to move the organization closer to achieving the big, hairy, audacious vision. The leader must own and drive it to completion, for if she doesn't, no one will, and it simply becomes another failed dream.

The vision must be shared. The leadership team must believe in it and pursue it relentlessly, along with the leader herself. The creation of the vision can be a team effort. Indeed, this can help get buy-in. Ultimate responsibility for the vision cannot, however, be delegated. The leader must own it, articulate it, repeat constantly, drive it relentlessly, and she must insist that others do the same. If they do not, they cannot be part of the team. A leader cannot yield on this. "Stubborn on vision; flexible on details."

If, in our large company, a leader or a manager went off on a lark and thought about engaging in conduct or took action that conflicted with the vision and the Four Pillars, they put their job at risk. As in all large organizations, unfortunately, that did happen on occasion, and the consequences were swift.

Our vision and the Four Pillars pushed us to make countless decisions to improve our profitability. They compelled us to develop consumer tires that meet the wants and needs of the end-user, and to improve our already very good service in our network of tire and automotive service stores. As discussed later, they required us to create numerous mentoring, development, and leadership programs so we could truly be a premier place to work. And they empowered us to be an outstanding corporate citizen. The specific actions we implemented and described throughout this book were an effort to achieve our vision. The actions we took to "relentlessly drive" our vision were ubiquitous and impacted every facet of the organization.

Change begins with leadership. That is, a trustworthy leader who is prepared to act. That leader must also articulate a clear and compelling vision that is bold, energizes the team, and aligns their actions. It gives the team hope that the future holds something better than today; something to strive for and accomplish together. A leader must articulate the future state, and a leader must repeat the vision at every opportunity, insist that other key members of the team do the same, and drive it to a reality.

The vision and Four Pillars gave Bridgestone Americas that direction and helped to ensure that we were all rowing the boat in the same direction. That is essential in every change effort. Why? As Yogi Berra said, "If you don't know where you're going, you'll end up someplace else."

7

Culture: Lesson #3

"Culture eats strategy for breakfast."

– Peter Drucker

"I WANT TO talk to you about worker safety . . . Every year, numerous Alcoa workers are injured so badly that they miss a day of work . . . I intend to make Alcoa the safest company in America. I intend to go for zero injuries." This is what Paul O'Neill, the new CEO of Alcoa who was brought in to turn around the old-line manufacturing company in 1987, said to a team of Wall Street investors in a press conference. One attendee pressed him, asking what was his business strategy to improve the company's financials? O'Neill retorted, "I'm not certain you heard me. If you want to understand how Alcoa is doing, you need to look at our workplace safety figures."

Investors had expected O'Neill to announce some concrete business strategies that would turn around the company, such as reducing inventories to improve cash flow or the like. Rather, the new CEO focused on safety. One attendee called back to his office and advised investors to sell their stock, saying the board had hired a hippie who would kill the company.[1]

Paul O'Neill did not kill the company. He put in place an extensive series of processes to focus on and improve worker safety. These processes enabled and even forced discussions throughout the ranks, in many cases up to him personally, on how safety could be improved. It worked. Over time, employees at every level started speaking up and talking about how they could improve workplace safety. But then, after being outspoken on safety related issues, employees started speaking up about all kinds of needed improvements. They drove excellence in different aspects of the business. Alcoa's financial performance improved dramatically, with net income growing fivefold during O'Neill's decade plus as CEO.

Interestingly, Alcoa's safety record was already pretty good, particularly for a heavy manufacturing operation. The CEO, though, created a crisis, or perhaps a rallying point: to be the safest company in America. Certainly, an audacious vision. No doubt safety was extremely important to O'Neill, as it should be for every executive. But I am also certain that he brilliantly used safety as a cultural change lever to drive excellence throughout the organization. He created a culture of excellence, and that is why the company's fortunes turned around.

The bottom line is this: "Culture isn't part of the game. It is the game," said Lou Gerstner who turned around IBM in the 1990s. I couldn't agree more.

* * *

But what exactly is corporate or organizational culture? There are many definitions, but most seem to focus solely on the way employees interact with one another.

---

[1] Rodd Wagner, "Have We Learned the Alcoa Keystone Habit Lesson," *Forbes*, January 22, 2019.

Culture certainly impacts what is and is not acceptable conduct as employees interact with one another. Culture largely dictates whether managers (taken as a whole) yell, micromanage, or belittle others or whether such behavior is unacceptable. A company whose culture is fast and loose ethically or legally is certainly more likely to find itself shrouded in legal problems than a company that follows the law and regulations seriously. Employees in the latter type of company know they put their career, reputation, and perhaps even their freedom on the line if they operate outside the bounds of the law. This is all reflected in the company's values, not necessarily those that are written (although they should be), but those that the company embraces through its practices.

A definition of culture that centers solely on how employees interact is, therefore, too narrow. Culture not only dictates "the way" things are done, but it also determines, at least to a large extent, what is done and how employees interact with customers, suppliers, and the rest of the outside world.

Four Seasons Hotels are known for outstanding service. If you ask a Four Seasons employee a question, they stop what they are doing, smile, and earnestly ask, "How can I help you." It is the company's culture, and it not only dictates how employees behave, but the specific actions they then take to make their guests happy.

Walmart's strategy is centered on low prices for just about everything one can buy. Its stores are staffed differently than a Neiman Marcus department store. Walmart's culture engrains frugality in its operations and is one of the ways it can sell products at such low prices.[2] That is part of its culture just as Alcoa used safety and, with it, striving for excellence, to be its driving cultural traits.

Bridgewater, one of the most successful investment firms in the world, stresses intense data analytics and complete

---

[2] It is worth pointing out that while Walmart is frugal in many ways, it is extraordinary in its efforts to address climate change.

transparency and candor. The candor, it has been reported, can be brutal in its honesty. But these practices allow it to make the very best investment decisions that it can possibly make, and these practices are surely a huge part of its culture.

A company's core business strategy also, if properly executed, becomes part of its culture. Think of Four Seasons and Disney for outstanding guest experiences; Apple and Google for innovation. These strategies are inseperable from their cultures.

So, culture is more than just how employees interact with each other. It substantially, if not wholly, determines what is done. Edgar Schein defines culture as "the sum total of everything an organization has learned in its history in dealing with external problems."[3]

Schein might be correct, but in search of a more specific definition, I define the amorphous concept of culture as the following:

Culture is the sum of the company's vision, values, strategy and spoken as well as unspoken rules of behavior which dictate the way employees behave and how they handle both internal and external issues.

If a company professes to be customer focused, yet when push comes to shove yields to other values, like ending a shift on time, then employees will frequently disappoint its customers. If a company claims to be innovative yet punishes when ideas don't pan out, it will squash the innovation engine. If a company claims it values courage and candor, yet managers act with contempt when someone makes a suggestion they don't care for, there will not be open discussions. Behaviors must be aligned to the vision, values, and policies or the culture will take on a life of its own. More on this in the chapter on alignment.

* * *

---

[3] Tim Kuppler interview published in *Leadership & Change*, 2015, https://www.leadershipandchangemagazine.com/edgar-schein-on-culture/

Against this backdrop and the above definition of what culture is, Bridgestone Americas consisted of good, well-meaning, devoted people. Our teammates are, as are all employees in any organization, a product of their environment. What the company focuses on is what becomes important to the people. We were very proud of our culture for doing the right thing, and helping our communities, which drove, among other things, strong local relations, and a positive reputation in those communities. But we needed more if we were going to take the company to the next level. We encouraged people to speak up, but, for some reason, people often didn't. Our structure of 21 "companies" (actually divisions) created in the early 1990s to help the integration of Firestone into Bridgestone was the right decision in its day. But over time it reduced communication among teammates in different parts of the organization. Many of our managers were excellent, but we still needed them to drive higher-performance expectations throughout the organization.

We were excellent at giving the car companies what they wanted in tires. But that wasn't always the same thing that the end-user wanted in her tires. Accordingly, I attempted to redefine our "customers" away from the car companies to the end-user. But try as we might, we couldn't change our corporate mindset that had been ingrained in our people for the entirety of their careers with the company. "Customers" were those companies that purchased tires directly from Bridgestone Americas. That was the car companies, tire wholesalers, and tire retailers. It was Bridgestone Americas' personality, and one's personality is both hard to see objectively and even harder to change.

It was who we were. It was in our DNA. It was our culture. Yet, we had to find a way to broaden our perspective if we were going to evolve.

We needed to open our mind to the possibility that there were other ways to think, other business models to follow, and other tactics and strategies that could be more successful than what had been done.

As CEO, it was my job to change this paradigm and get one and all to see broader possibilities, or better yet, excited to embrace new cultural traits.

I first focused on getting the most influential leaders in the organization on board. The newly formed Executive Committee was intended to address the most important issues facing the company. As explained in the chapter on leadership, the Executive Committee created its Rules of Engagement, including Be Present (that is, no texting or emails during the meetings), State Your Views (committee members were expected to participate and contribute), Speak with One Voice (once a decision was made all members fully supported it when the meeting was over). These rules were printed on a poster board, and we reviewed them at the start of each meeting and put on display around the room for all to see throughout the meetings.

Yet, words on a board are meaningless until they come alive in the interactions of the people around the table and after they leave the meeting room. Our people knew their respective businesses very well. They were smart, experienced, and capable. We just had to get them interacting more with each other and exploring new ways of doing things with the goal of taking our company to the next level.

We worked hard to create a safe environment so an executive wasn't worried that a comment would get their legs cut out from under them. I knew it would take time for the team to trust me and the new COO, but I also knew that if we stayed the course, if we listened actively, welcomed ideas, encouraged discussion, and expressed appreciation when someone had the courage to disagree with us, the trust would come. And, over several meetings it did.

I also knew that it was one thing for an Executive Committee member to disagree with me and the COO. That would happen in the fullness of time as people realized I truly welcomed different perspectives. The litmus test of our culture change founded in courage and candor, however, would be for one executive to openly disagree with the business strategy of another executive, a colleague, who also was in the room, and to do so in front of me. That took significantly longer to achieve.

Changing the culture in the Executive Committee meetings was only the beginning, though. It wasn't enough that the 10 or so members of the committee engaged in true debate and actively listened to one another in closed door sessions. The culture in the broader organization needed to change as well. That was a far more daunting challenge.

* * *

Edgar Schein, Professor Emeritus with MIT Sloan School of Management, is considered one of the early scholars and leading authorities on organization culture. Professor Schein councils that one of the challenges in working with culture in today's organization is that the focus on culture is just that, only about the culture. Instead, he argues the focus needs to be on solving business problems that help drive the cultural transformation. Much like what Paul O'Neill did at Alcoa, we needed a cultural change lever that made sense for the business issues we were struggling with. The question was what would be our cultural change lever?

A few members of the Executive Committee argued that we should use customer service as the cultural change lever. But that made little sense to me as Bridgestone already provided great customer service to the car companies and tire dealers, who we defined as our customer. Our efforts to explain to the organization that the end-user also was our customer just wasn't getting traction. So, in my view, using customer service as the culture change lever would take us to no place different.

If we were going to achieve our goals, we needed new and creative ideas. So, after some debate, the Executive Committee decided that innovation would be the business issue we would focus on, and we would use it as the change lever to drive a new culture throughout the company.

To kick off this initiative, we scheduled a two-day offsite meeting with the company's top 150 executives. Certainly, no such meeting like this had occurred at Bridgestone Americas in decades. Because of the company's vast size (55,000 employees) and scope (different businesses operating on five continents) the goal was to get this team marching to the beat of a new drummer (that is, alignment); they, in turn, would help drive the changes further down in the organization. The vice president of Talent, Organization, and Culture designed the meeting. It surpassed all my expectations.

I opened the meeting, explaining that we had a problem. Our two major brands – Bridgestone and Firestone – would stand up favorably against competitive tires from a quality and performance perspective. One need only look at our incomparable Indy Racing tires, or that many truckers, farmers, and mining companies who spent large sums on tires that were critical to their business placed their faith in our products. Yet, on the consumer side of the business, our tires were neither the most recognizable nor the most highly regarded by many consumers. Because of this, one of our competitors could command the top price point and we had to price our tires below theirs. At the same time, over the previous several years, low-priced tires from Asia (particularly from China) were flooding our markets, driving prices lower across the board. As a result, Bridgestone's margins were being squeezed.

I said we had two fundamental choices. One, we could substantially lower costs, and try to compete largely on price. To do that, costs would have to be cut to the bones. No one would enjoy that process and many wouldn't survive it, and at the end of the day, it still would be highly unlikely that we could beat the Chinese at their game. In other words, if this was our strategy going forward, we would likely fail.

The second option was to become the most innovative company in the industry. If successful, we could command a premium price point. I explained further that this had been discussed in the Executive Committee, and the committee concluded this was our best course of action.

I further explained that being innovative was not just about coming up with the next miracle drug, if you will. It was about far more than just hitting home runs with new products or services. Indeed, market changing tire technologies are extraordinarily rare and difficult to come by. Innovation meant hitting singles and doubles. It had to permeate everything we did. We had to be innovative in figuring out exactly what the different categories of end-users wanted, how to improve our supply chain, and HR programs. In other words, innovation had to be the driving force in everything we did, from our internal processes and policies to our products, services, and marketing, to the way we helped make the communities we worked in be better places to live. Innovation had to become Bridgestone Americas' way of business, its lifeblood as a company.

There were many questions after I finished addressing the executives in the room and, before leaving the stage, I did my best to answer them. That had now become a big part of Bridgestone's culture: encouraging questions and answering them with honesty and transparency.

After answering questions, I introduced Ram Charan, a former Harvard Business School faculty, an author of many business and leadership books including at least one on innovation, and one of the most sought-after consultants in the world. Ram explained how innovation worked at some of the most successful companies in the world. He said the most innovative companies focused on who he called the Boss – the end-user of the products and services. This intense focus allowed a company to understand at profound levels the spoken and unspoken wants and needs of the Boss, and this insight then provoked ideas (innovations) to try to meet those needs.

He also emphasized both the corporate culture and processes that are needed to foster innovation. Along the way, he answered virtually every question that was thrown at him. And there were a lot of questions.

Six hours later, when he was done and I'm sure exhausted, I returned to the stage: "I have just one question for you," I said.

"Do you think our culture will allow us to do what is needed to be truly innovative?" Throughout the team of 150 executives, the answer was no, it wouldn't.

I agreed with them, saying, "Tomorrow you will come back to this room. We will break into teams of 10, and with the help of outside facilitators, you will design our cultural blueprint so that we can become the most innovative company in our industry."

The next day, the COO and I sat on the sidelines and let the facilitators and teams do their work. Each team first debated and then collected their views on what our cultural blueprint should look like and with the help of the facilitators the various ideas were then synthesized into one document. But I had made it clear to the lead facilitator that three things had to be in the cultural blueprint.

1. We had to focus on the end-user, that is, the Boss, in addition to the car companies.
2. We had to more fully embrace courage and candor to create an environment that recognized good ideas come from anywhere, so all ideas, debates, etc. were not only welcome, but expected.
3. We had to be inclusive, meaning all the right people had to be at the table before decisions were made. We had to improve our communications if we were going to take the company to the next level.

By the end of that second day, the group had done its job. They selected a few people to present their conclusions to us on behalf of, and in front of, the full group. What they came up with was fabulous and they called it the Rules of the Road.

The photo on the right (Figure 7.2) is the actual flipchart where the team wrote out the seven rules of Bridgestone's new cultural blueprint. At the suggestion of an HR executive, every person in the room signed the draft, symbolizing each person's commitment to live and drive this culture throughout the organization.

The image on the left (Figure 7.1) is a re-created version of the Rules of the Road. The only difference from the original draft

Bridgestone Americas

RULES OF THE ROAD

1. Boss Is #1
2. Drive Innovation
3. Courage and Candor
4. Inclusiveness and Collaboration
5. Listen Actively
6. One Voice
7. Walk the Talk

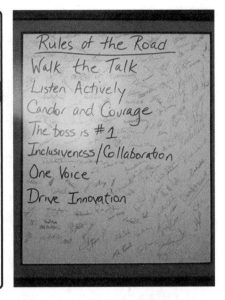

Figure 7.1 Bridgestone Americas' Rules of the Road

Figure 7.2 The Seven Rules That Made Up Bridgestone's New Cultural Blueprint

is the team revised the order of the rules. Laminated cards printed with the Rules of the Road were later handed out to each leader in the organization.

The Rules of the Road are as follows:

1. **The Boss Is #1.** Bridgestone Americas would continue to provide great service to our "original equipment" customers, that is, the car companies, as they were very important to us. From that point forward, we also would develop a new and profound understanding of the wants and needs of the end-user of our products, and we would always make sure we were giving the end-user, the Boss, what they wanted from our products. That relationship would help ensure our products and services met the Boss' expectations and allow us to develop innovative products and services to meet the wants and needs of the Boss. This concept took to the organization like wildfire. Thereafter, when I took plant tours, it was not

uncommon for factory line workers to say, "Mr. Garfield, let me show you what I'm doing for the Boss."

2. **Drive Innovation**. Innovation, as our outside expert explained to the team, typically is not an accident. It is an intentional, focused, and deliberative process. If Bridgestone Americas was truly going to become innovative, we had to have a deliberate process driving it forward, and each leader had to do what they could to make it happen. Moreover, we had to be innovative not just in our products and services, but in our internal processes and in everything we did. We called it "everyday innovations," meaning everyone should always be thinking about how they could continuously improve what they did every day. And so, as discussed in Chapter 9 on alignment, we created a company-wide innovation process.

3. **Courage and Candor**. Innovation, and for that matter simply good business, will not happen unless people operate with courage and candor – speaking up, stating their views, challenging each other, and speaking the truth. For this to happen, leaders and managers must create an atmosphere that both allows and encourages others to speak up. Indeed, this is an essential part of good business because good ideas can indeed come from anywhere.

4. **Inclusiveness and Collaboration**. Innovation will not happen without the right people at the table. Good business also won't happen without the necessary people at the table so the right hand and left hand are on the same page. In all our decisions and projects, the right people had to be at the table.

5. **Listen Actively**. Active listening is an important element of creating an atmosphere where people feel that they are being heard and it is safe to speak their minds. In other words, make sure you understand before trying to be understood.

6. **One Voice**. If we were going to be innovative and take our performance to the next level, we could not say one thing in a meeting, and then do something different when the meeting

ended. In other words, passive-aggressive behavior would not be tolerated.

7. **Walk the Talk**. We couldn't just say these words. We had to live it, be it, relentlessly drive it. We actually had to do what we said we were going to do.

We were thrilled with the results. We told the team how proud we were of their extraordinary work. We also vowed that this was not the last of these executive off-site meetings. They would be held twice a year to help drive the company culture and business further.

Perhaps most importantly, I informed the group that if the COO or I ever deviated from the Rules of the Road, anyone had the right to call us out for our lapse. But by the same token, from that point forward I could say to others when the need arose, "You created these rules, not me. You must live by your own Rules of the Road that you created."

* * *

A business-driven change lever is used to create, define, and drive new behaviors. In Bridgestone Americas' case, it was manifested in the Rules of the Road.

Innovation and the Rules of the Road created Bridgestone Americas' true north. We knew where we had to go, and the team was energized about the new direction and the possibilities for the future. The cultural change lever – innovation – was something the entire organization rallied around, strived for, and enthusiastically supported. Most importantly, it was not randomly selected but rather addressed a strategic need, greater innovation.

To emphasize the importance innovation was to play in the future of the company, it was added to the Four Pillars. The vision of being the leader in our industries stayed the same. So, in fact, did each of the Four Pillars, which were discussed earlier. We said that innovation was foundational to achieving our vision.

VISION: OUSTANDING CONTRIBUTOR TO BS GROUP AND THE LEADER IN OUR INDUSTRIES

BRIDGESTONE AMERICAS

FINANCIALLY SUCCESSFUL	BRAND PROMISE	PREMIER PLACE TO WORK	OUTSTANDING CORPORATE CITIZEN
5% ROA IN 2012	PRODUCTS AND SERVICES MUST MEET OR EXCEED USER EXPECTATIONS	ATTRACT, RETAIN, AND DEVELOP LEADERS WHO SHARE IN OUR VISION	LIVING THE BRIDGESTONE WAY
NA TIRE SUSTAINABLE PROFITS			

INNOVATION IN EVERYTHING WE DO

Figure 7.3   The Revised Four Pillars

Everything we do, internally and customer facing, was to be driven by innovation. The new image of the Four Pillars is seen in Figure 7.3.

The hardest part, though, was before us; that was to actually make the Rules of the Road Bridgestone Americas' culture, day in and day out. Saying we needed to be innovative, putting the Rules of the Road down on paper, and adding innovation as the foundation of the Four Pillars slide did little to change behaviors and habits. The pronouncement of the goal doesn't generate results. It takes a lot of hard work, focus, and determination. Making innovation and the Rules of the Road come alive was no different.

We had to align our process, policies, and practices with the concept of innovation. Much of this is discussed in the following chapters, but one of the many programs we developed to drive innovation was a daylong session called Creating an Innovative Culture. It was designed to help turn our leaders into teachers. Our senior leaders partnered with HR to roll out the innovative culture throughout the organization. We met in groups of 50 in hotels across the country to roll out our new cultural blueprint.

The goal – make sure every employee understood the reasons behind the new cultural blueprint, the importance of innovation, what each of the Rules of the Road stood for, how innovation happens, and what was expected of them.

We acted as swiftly as we reasonably could on many fronts, but it still took time. It was not something that could be clicked on like a light switch. Rather, that was just the beginning. It took months and years of hard work to be the kind of organization, realize the vision, and establish the culture we had worked for.

At the end of day, people make the culture come alive. Driving the cultural change meant both helping people alter their behaviors and holding their feet to the fire at the same time. Some people and groups adopted quicker than others. There were lapses that had to be addressed. Some people couldn't make the change and so we had to make a change. Much of this and more is discussed in the next chapter on people.

We also had to create policies and processes to drive innovation and to make the Rules of the Road come alive. Without this alignment, we would be saying one thing, but our policies and processes would drive us a different way. And then, of course, we needed to execute, what we call *focused execution*. In our everyday actions and decisions, we had to, as Jack Welch put it, "relentlessly drive" the results we were seeking through innovation and the Rules of the Road. We could not let up for if we did, our behaviors, mindset, and decisions would resort to the habits of old.

We all had much to learn, and at times we fumbled our way through it. Changing the culture in a large organization takes years. There were setbacks at times to be sure. But overall, the progress was continually encouraging. Persistence pays off, and we were nothing if not persistent.

8

People: Lesson #4

"You can design and create, and build the most wonderful place in the world. But it takes people to make the dream a reality."

– *Walt Disney*

ON MORE THAN one occasion, the COO or I would meet with a well-liked, high-performing executive to inform that individual they were being let go. The reason: they weren't the right cultural fit for the organization we envisioned. We would thank them for their service and contributions to the company, sincerely wished them well and said goodbye. A member of the HR team would then take over and present them with their severance package. Early on, this was a shock for the organization.

For me, letting someone go, for just about any reason shy of unethical, inappropriate, or illegal conduct, was the worst part of managing others and leading a group and an organization. I hated it. But as much as I hated to do this, the decision also was usually straightforward. If we were going to achieve our goals, we had to have the right people in the right roles, and if an individual was not a good cultural fit for the organization, I had to act. In such situations, the organization came to expect it.

Business is a team sport. Having the right people in the right positions is critical for success. Hiring, firing, and promotion decisions are among the most important any businessperson can make. This is true for start-ups and mature companies, conglomerates, and small operations, non-profits, and for-profit ventures. People loom large. Indeed, no less than Bill Gates[1] and the late Steve Jobs[2] attribute much of their success to hiring the best people they could find.

As important as people are in an organization's success during stable times, massive change accentuates their importance. Change is a team sport as well. In some ways, perhaps, even more so. As explained earlier, and without a doubt, meaningful change will not happen without a leader's action, persistence, and determination. But change also cannot happen without the support of every key member of the team. The leadership team and other key individuals either support the change efforts or they do not. There is no in-between, no half-way. When supporting the changes, they help reduce fear and resistance to change, and they can help make the tide of change overwhelming. When a change effort is not supported by key leaders, change is doomed. Negative behavior, whether overt or passive-aggressive, is a cancer in the organization that metastasizes if allowed to remain in the corporate body.

We spent considerable time, energy, and money building support for the many changes we sought to make. That alone, however, was not enough.

We had to have the right people in the right roles. That meant making people changes where we thought it was needed, whether for cultural or substantive issues. It also meant setting high expectations, investing in people, and delegating properly. We learned much about each of these areas, which will be discussed in this chapter.

---

[1] David Bradford, "What I Learned From: Bill Gates," *LinkedIn*, July 2, 2015.
[2] Marcel Schwantes, "Steve Jobs Said There's 1 Decision that Separates Leaders Who Achieve Success From Those Who Still Don't Get It," *Inc.*, December 10, 2018.

But make no mistake: Bridgestone Americas' success is attributable to an outstanding team that both supported and advanced the changes we were driving and who were extremely capable in their jobs. Had we not put such a team in place, our changes would have failed, pure and simple.

The Right Team

Steve Jobs and Bill Gates didn't achieve their respective enormous successes by being wrong most of the time. Both have said that a key to their success was hiring the smartest people they could find. Jobs explained his rationale: "A small team of A plus players can run circles around a giant team of B and C players."[3] No one can argue with the results of either of these extraordinary business leaders.

But is hiring A-plus players just about hiring the smartest people one can find? For some companies, perhaps. For others, smarts alone do not define an "A" player. There is more to it than that.

While flying some years ago, I had a conversation with a passenger sitting next to me. He said he had just joined the Walt Disney Company as a senior executive in its security group. He had been with the FBI for over 25 years, stationed at various field offices around the world.

During the conversation, the passenger asked, "Guess how many interviews I had to go through before Disney hired me?" Stumped, I threw out eight or nine interviews, or thereabouts. His answer: "Nineteen. Nineteen different interviews before Disney would hire me." He knew security, he said, having been a seasoned veteran of the FBI. That wasn't the issue. The issue was culture. Disney wanted to make certain he could do his security job while being a good fit for the culture Disney creates and

---

[3] Krista Bradford, "Recruit A Players/Steve Jobs Quote," *The Good Search*, May 21, 2019.

embraces for both its guests and employees. For Disney, culture was nonnegotiable, and Disney is one of those companies that seems to get a lot right.

Zappos took a similar hiring strategy to Disney, although its tactics for ensuring a good cultural fit were very different. The online shoe store was founded in 1999, with start-up costs of roughly $2 million. Zappos eventually expanded to selling clothes and handbags. Just 10 years after its founding, Zappos was sold to Amazon for roughly $1 billion. Not a bad return on the initial investment. One of Zappos's secrets: it hires for culture.

As we at Bridgestone Americas were making efforts to redefine the culture within the organization, a former Zappos human resource executive was invited to speak with our senior executive team at one of our off-site meetings. This is how the hiring process at Zappos was described to us.

Zappos is headquartered in Las Vegas. When an out of towner arrives in Vegas for an interview, a car is waiting at the airport to take the interviewee to the company headquarters, and it returns that person to the airport at the end of the interview process. The company then reaches out to the driver to ask what that person was like. Were they outgoing? Friendly? Rude? Polite? Dismissive or any other impressions? Zappos wants to know what that person is like when they aren't on the interview stage.

That was just the beginning. If that person gets hired, they go through a three-week training process to learn about the job, the company, its expectations, and particularly its culture. After investing three weeks educating its new hire, Zappos then does something truly unique: it offers to pay that person $2,000 to leave the company. Yes, that's right. After investing the time and money interviewing, hiring, and then training a person, Zappos will pay someone good money to walk away from the company right then and there.

It's rationale: after those three weeks, the person now understands what Zappos is about and what it is like to work there. If it isn't a good cultural fit, that person should know it by then, and better for that person to leave then instead of later after that person has taken a toll on the Zappos culture. That is hiring for culture. Culture is everything.

Every organization and team must decide what are the key characteristics for its team members. Is it capability, experience, intelligence, culture, all the above, or something else? This decision is critical and should guide promoting, hiring, and firing decisions.

At Bridgestone Americas, we learned to be greedy. We wanted both excellent capability and a great culture fit. We assessed our people on both.

Over my tenure, we made extensive people changes, sometimes because of capability and other times because some could not or would not support or adapt to the cultural or other changes being made. Six years into the change journey at Bridgestone Americas, roughly three-fifths of the top 150 executives in the company had not been in their positions when my tenure began.

Some of the top executives were promoted from within and we had to fill the positions they vacated. Others were let go either because they could not do the job up to our standards or they could not advance the culture we were trying to create, and still others retired. These were often tough and even painful decisions, but ultimately, for the company we were working so hard to take to the next level, the right decision.

To fill vacant positions, sometimes we promoted from within and sometimes we hired from the outside, both of which have their pros and cons. Some of the moves proved outstanding, others not so much. In such cases, we made more changes.

Promoting from Within versus Hiring from the Outside

It was rare for Bridgestone Americas to hire a senior executive from the outside, at least until I became CEO. That changed early on when we decided we needed a new chief marketing officer. Like many old-line manufacturing companies, not much emphasis was placed on marketing. Indeed, many manufacturing companies converted engineers to marketers rather than hiring individuals with extensive training and experience in marketing.

Shortly after me and the new COO assumed our positions, I informed human resources that we needed an experienced, classically trained marketer to rebuild our marketing strategy and programs. We had not used an executive search firm previously, so HR began by selecting a firm to help recruit the right person. The search firm sent us many resumes to review and with their help, the list was whittled down to a handful of candidates. But none of the interviewees were overly impressive. The recruiting firm advised us that if we wanted better candidates, we would need to increase our compensation package.

Disappointed, we got on the phone with one of our key outside advisors who forcefully urged us not to settle for anything less than an "A" candidate. Simple and logical advice, but we explained our problem. Bridgestone Americas' pay structure apparently would not entice top notch people to join the company, and even if we managed to land one, we doubted we'd keep such a person for the long haul. His response was quick and spot on: You either want to raise the bar or you don't; you either want great people or you don't. "Forget about your rigid pay structure," he said. "When you find the right person, get creative and structure a compensation package for that person. Companies do that all the time." And, he finished, "If that person's financial demands are ridiculous and out of line with reality, then you probably don't have the right person for the job."

As for keeping such a person for the long term, he asked if we would rather have a superstar for five years and if and when that superstar leaves, find another superstar, or would we rather have a "B" player for life? You make the company better by hiring "A" players, he reiterated. Moreover, if the work is challenging and the company is a good place to work, who knows. Maybe that person will stay for the long haul.

He persuaded us. We did not settle. Ultimately, we hired a terrific executive and marketer to rebuild our marketing team.

He repositioned some people to better fit their skill sets and hired other very smart, talented classically trained marketers. Through that process he built a marketing team that was not only in a class by itself in the global Bridgestone organization, but a team that could stand up favorably to any in the industry. Indeed, it was through their considerable talents and efforts that we rebuilt the Firestone brand (discussed in more detail later). Moreover, the new executive's leadership style, as well as the leadership styles of the people he hired, advanced the all-important cultural changes we were making.

With the advisor's guidance echoing in our minds, our entire hiring approach changed. We started recruiting top executives from world-renowned companies. It was not just about capability. We had to change the culture to fit the Rules of the Road and the people we hired had to help us make that change; otherwise, our efforts would die on the vine.

We put candidates through a host of interviews throughout the company so we could get feedback from people with different perspectives. Additionally, before hiring candidates for our most senior positions, that same outside advisor, a trained psychologist, interviewed them for several hours in New York and put them through a battery of tests. His input was critical to us.

To further improve our outside hiring, we partnered with Barton Executive Search, a small, boutique firm in Atlanta. We did not seem to be enough of a priority for some of the more well-known firms. Barton Executive Search took the time to truly understand our organization, the business, the changes we were making, and our cultural needs. The firm and our HR group put enormous energy into ensuring that the candidates we were looking for were good fits for the organization.

This was expensive and time consuming, to be sure. But the investment in people, if you will, paid off enormously. I am certain that but for that investment, I would not have a story to tell.

* * *

Whether to hire from the outside or promote from within is a dilemma most organizations face. For the first few years of my tenure as CEO, Bridgestone Americas relied far more heavily on outside hires than on internal promotions. This was controversial within the organization, but there were several reasons for this approach.

First, if we were going take the company to the next level, we needed completely new ideas, new strategies, and new ways of doing things. One way to propel this process is to hire people from the outside who had different experiences than we had. Our hope was that these hires would bring new and very different strategies to the table. And many did. It would have taken time for the existing team to learn what the most successful companies in the world were doing and then try to implement it at Bridgestone Americas. We believed it was faster to transplant those concepts into our organization by way of the people we recruited.

Second, in a few cases, we simply did not have the level of substantive expertise we thought was needed to take the company to a new level of performance. As mentioned, like many old-line manufacturers, we had not placed much emphasis on marketing. So, our marketing team, while wonderful people who worked hard, generally did not consist of classically trained marketers. We wanted the internal capability to build and create modern day, sophisticated marketing strategies and campaigns and then effectively execute them. Hiring from the outside to rebuild the marketing team was crucial to achieve this and proved a resounding success.

Finally, if new hires were chosen wisely, it would jump start the crucial cultural transformation by bringing in people who worked in cultures similar to what we were trying to build rather than promoting individuals who would have to learn and adapt to a new culture while taking over a new job.

One of Bridgestone's large truck tire customers was PACCAR, which produces the highly regarded Peterbilt and Kenworth trucks. Many years ago, PACCAR's then president explained to me that the company had decided to relocate its engineering operations to a new state. Many of the company's engineers refused to make the move and so the company had to rebuild its engineering team largely from scratch, a scary proposition to be sure. Yet by doing so, he said, the company was able to change the team's culture almost overnight, and that proved critical to the company's long-term success.

With these thoughts in mind, for roughly two years, many of the most significant positions in Bridgestone were filled from the outside. A new head of marketing along with a stable of outstanding new talent under him. We hired someone from Kimberly-Clark to run our North American consumer group, one of our largest business units. In relatively short order, he was promoted to COO. To fill his existing position as head of the North American consumer group, we hired an individual from Pfizer. We went outside to hire a new president for the retail store network, for the Latin American tire operations, and for our operations in Brazil. We also hired new vice presidents for human resources and purchasing.

It all had the desired effect. The new blood brought new ideas, strategies, and a renewed energy to their teams and the broader company, and without a doubt they helped accelerate the cultural change. Those who joined Bridgestone Americas also hired wonderfully talented people to work for them. They, and so many others, were outstanding individuals who helped to make us an even better company than we had been.

We didn't always get the hiring right. Whether substantively or culturally, some of our hires fell short. It is impossible for any company to bat a 100 percent in its hiring and, for that matter, in its internal promotion decisions. When it turns out a mistake is made, it is important to correct it promptly, first by giving the person a reasonable opportunity to improve and if that fails then filling the position with someone else. Better to admit the mistake than perpetuate the mistake.

Our fear that "A" players might not stay with the company for an extended period turned out not to be much of a concern. Many did stay. With the new culture, energy and opportunities to develop and implement new strategies, the work was exciting and challenging, and their views and leadership were welcome and appreciated. Further, Nashville is a wonderful, vibrant place to live and raise a family. Finally, we tailored our compensation packages to get the talent we needed to grow the business. For those who did move on, because of the strong bench they had built and the new leadership programs we had put in place, we usually had in-house people ready to step up to the next level. If we didn't, we went outside as we had done before. And the company moved forward.

* * *

Some people argued that we were making a mistake hiring so heavily from the outside. They argued, among other things, that because we knew the internal person better, we would have a better idea what we were getting. But that equation is not so simple.

In certain situations, promoting from within is less risky. One has a deeper understanding of the work habits, leadership style, intelligence, and other capabilities of the internal candidate versus the outside candidate. Plus, the internal candidate knows the organization, its people, and the culture, and so is arguably better able to have an immediate impact.

But those facts can cut both ways. Internal candidates are, at least in part, a product of the thinking, strategies, and culture in which they have worked. Will the internal candidate bring something new to the table – a new strategy, perspective, ideas, and the new positive cultural traits, or will the person continue the same old, same old? As the great American renaissance man and Founding Father Benjamin Franklin said, "When you're finished changing, you're finished."

A person should rarely, if ever, be promoted to continue what was always done. When driving change within a team or organization, the question must be asked, "What change will the internal candidate bring to the table?" Sometimes quite a bit. The individual who led the Bridge to Excellence discussed in the previous chapter became our chief financial officer, and he transformed our finance function from transactionally focused into a strategic business partner. Another individual who had been the controller took over our IT group and again transformed that operation. But other times, perhaps not so much.

Additionally, there is a tendency to believe that someone who is a star in their current role will succeed at the next level as well. But all too often that is not the case. Different skills and perspectives are required as a person advances in their career. Thus, Babe Ruth never managed the Yankees or any other team.

The various transitions that exist in a large organization are discussed at length in the outstanding book *The Leadership Pipeline*. Does the internal candidate (and this is certainly true of the external candidate as well) have the necessary skills, perspective, and values to succeed in the role under consideration? In my experience, there tends to be a bias of "yes" for internal candidates, but that bias might be a disservice to the company and the internal candidate as well.

Going from a doer to a manager of others is not an easy step. Being great at doing something doesn't necessarily translate into being great at managing others. Babe Ruth was the best baseball "doer" of all time, but no owner believed he could translate that into managing others. Conversely, Bill Belichick, very arguably the greatest football coach ever, was not good enough to play (that is, be a "doer") in the NFL. Someone who manages doers might not be great at managing and leading managers of doers. A leader of other managers may not do well at developing broader strategies for their part of the organization and coordinating those strategies with other parts of the organization, both necessary skills as someone moves up the organizational ladder.

A consulting client asked my thoughts about a potential promotion for a young, but very talented individual. The individual had recently been moved into her first sales role and was performing well. She was gregarious, smart, enthusiastic, and outgoing, and she was excited about the opportunity, so it seemed a good fit. But she was not experienced in many of the key aspects of what the new role would entail. Specifically, she had little experience managing people and in her new role she would run a business with hundreds of employees in various geographic locations. Moreover, she was new to that particular business and so had a huge learning curve in front of her.

After a deeper dive into the issue, I recommended against the promotion at that time. My primary consideration was the promotion was not fair to the individual. It would have been a significant leap to a very difficult job in a very difficult part of the business that had been struggling. To me, it seemed like a bridge too far. If that proved true, if she failed in the new role, then what? It would have been a disaster for her. I asked the client, would you demote her, let her go, or what? In my opinion, she needed more time to learn about that particular business, and how to both lead people, run a business in general and develop and implement strategies. I recommended that they put her under someone who could mentor her, and that is what the client ultimately did. This gave her the chance to continue her professional growth. In due course, her time would come, and she would almost certainly become a highly valued member of the senior executive team. But the giant step that was under consideration actually could end up setting her back.

The point is this, however: promotions are very big decisions that should not be taken lightly, not only for the organization but, just as importantly, out of great care and regard for the person being considered for a promotion. There usually is not a winner when someone is promoted to a stretch assignment and fails.

* * *

Our strategy to largely hire from the outside for the first few years had another consequence though. The morale of the existing employee base took a steep drop. They believed, understandably, there was little or no real future for them. To address this, we began to strike a better balance between new hires and internal promotions. Nevertheless, we would only hire or promote a candidate who we believed could perform up to our high expectations substantively and culturally. On that basic principle we never settled. We didn't always succeed, but we did the best we could. Perhaps as important, the message was delivered throughout the organization: high performance coupled with advancing our new culture were not negotiable.

Invest in People

Mature companies in tough industries usually do not have cash to burn. Competition is stiff, and such companies must make wise decisions on how to invest their money if they are to thrive, much less survive. As described earlier, the company went through an efficiency improvement and right-sizing effort called "Bridge to Excellence," which was discussed in the chapter on leadership.

But we did not "pocket" all our savings from the program. Rather, we invested some of that money back into people. All too often, when money gets tight, one of the first things to go is investments in people – so often called the soft stuff.

If we truly wanted to be a "Premier Place to Work" as set forth in the Four Pillars, and if we really wanted to change our corporate culture, we had to up our investment in our people.

This meant not only hiring and promoting outstanding individuals who would drive the business in new ways and advance our cultural changes, it also meant increasing our investment in cultural, managerial, leadership, and sales training throughout the organization.

To that end, HR developed a company-wide training program for all front-line managers. The day-long program focused on changing one's mindset from doing the work (micromanaging) to managing others who do the work. It emphasized, among other things, how to give feedback (positive and constructive) to one's direct reports and how to promote our new culture. This program was neither easy to develop nor inexpensive. But it was very important. It received rave reviews throughout the organization. It not only helped our managers be better at their jobs, but it also showed we wanted everyone to succeed.

This was just one of the several people development programs we invested in. As part of the cultural change efforts each of the top 30 or so executives in the organization was offered the opportunity to work with an executive coach at the company's expense. The coach's job was to help the executive be better at managing and leading their people while advancing the company's cultural directive, the Rules of the Road. This included such things like setting high expectations, giving effective feedback, avoiding micromanaging, working effectively with one's peers, creating an environment where others could and did speak up, and so on. That coach would be their confidant and advisor. The coach would not report back to anyone else.

For those executives who took us up on the offer and who were open to the process, it was of great value. They became better at their jobs, their teams became more engaged, and the company benefited significantly. There were others who either couldn't or wouldn't adopt the Rules of the Road, and for them we ultimately had to make a move.

HR developed another critical program, one to identify who were the best among our middle level and more junior talent, evaluate their strengths as well as their learning and experiential gaps, and then identify opportunities to fill those gaps. To do this each senior executive in the organization identified their most talented team members and then evaluated and graded them using a standardized methodology. Then there was an annual mandatory and exhaustive all-day, off-site meeting, where each senior executive shared their evaluations of their talent with the other senior executives in the room. Those executives in the room who had had meaningful exposure to the individuals being discussed would then give their opinions of the individual and, through a give and take, a list of the most promising talent was developed as well as which areas of the organization had talent gaps.

Using that list of our most promising leaders, we identified opportunities that could lead to a promotion or high-profile projects for those individuals to further their development, either within their existing team or in other teams. This not only created enthusiasm among our best and brightest, but it also made it clear that a particular team could not shield stars from other opportunities by blocking a move to another team within the organization, as happens in some organizations. Rather, the goal was to use the vast opportunities within the entire Bridgestone Americas organization to help develop our talent into outstanding executives.

Our investment in people did not end there. There was yet another all-day, off-site meeting with the senior executive team to discuss succession planning. Each executive discussed who they saw as their potential successors. Other executives then had the opportunity to comment on and even suggest others who might be prospective successors. The ultimate decision would not be theirs. Rather, the decision would be for the appropriate level of senior management. But the benefit was in the discussion. Potential successors were identified and what moves, experiences, or learnings those people would need to succeed if they were promoted were discussed. It was then HR and management's joint responsibility to ensure that we followed up on giving those promising executives the opportunities they needed to further their success.

As my predecessor wisely said many times, our competitors also have factories and tire building machines. What makes the difference is people. He could not have been more right. That concept is the easy part. The rubber meets the road in doing something about it, and that means investing in people's success. We put our money where our mouth was. In turn, the people we invested in wanted to show us that our investments were worthwhile, and most did this by doing their best to succeed.

"People Perform Up to the Level You Tolerate"[4]

"It's a funny thing about life; if you refuse to accept anything but the best, you very often will get it," said the author and play-wright W. Somerset Maugham.[5] Put another way, as a leader and a manager, you get what you tolerate. "It's not what you preach. It's what you tolerate."[6]

This is cynical, to be sure. Certainly, there are those who set such high-performance expectations for themselves that they will always deliver excellence. That is just who they are. But for many people the level of performance tolerated by leadership defines their performance.

Part of taking the company to the next level was setting higher-performance expectations and holding people to that standard. To do this we engaged a controversial strategy. We established parameters that only allowed a certain percentage of people within each group to receive the two highest performance

---

[4] Some years ago, I read an article in which a CEO was quoted as saying people perform up to the level one tolerates. I do not recall who made this insightful and provocative statement nor can I find that article. But whoever it was deserves the credit for this phrase, not me.

[5] Goodreads.com.

[6] Jocko Willink and Leif Babin, *Extreme Ownership: How the U.S. Navy Seals Lead and Win* (St. Martin's Press, 2015).

levels and mandated that a certain percentage would have to be rated in the two lowest levels of performance. In other words, we imposed grading on a curve. Further, if a person remained in the lowest two levels of performance for a specified time period, then that person would have to be removed from the organization. The goals were to force managers to adopt higher expectations for performance and to ensure that all managers would be honest with people about how they can do better.

Frankly, I do not care for the concept of forced grading on a mandated curve. But I could not think of another way to compel leaders to (1) set and enforce higher expectations and (2) ensure that they gave honest and constructive feedback to their people, something everyone both needs and is entitled to. We did this to get the organization to raise its game.

Some companies have done away with performance reviews altogether, and some employees urged that we do the same. In our view, that was not an option for us at the stage in our cultural change. We needed to set high expectations across the board and to fully ingrain the culture of giving completely honest feedback, whether negative or positive. If and when those cultural traits became sufficiently ingrained throughout the organization that we were as a matter of course setting high expectations and giving effective feedback, then, at that point, years down the road, perhaps we could be one of those companies that didn't need regular performance reviews. Instead, we would review each other's performance on a daily basis as it should be done. But we had to get there first.

Reviewing each other's performance, including the CEO's, was the ultimate intent. Ray Dalio founded Bridgewater, one of the world's most successful investment firms. One of his key principles, of which there are many, is radical truth and transparency. Blunt honesty and openness are key, and this applies to honesty and openness directed at the top dog, Dalio himself. In a YouTube video, Dalio displayed an email that he recently received, in which a person in his organization wrote to Ray that he "deserved a D- for [his] performance today in the meeting . . . you did not prepare at all because there is no way you could have been that disorganized. . . ."[7]

For many, it is a staggering idea that subordinates could send an email like that to the CEO. But for Ray Dalio, this radical transparency and truth is a critical part of creating an organization that constantly strives to make the very best decisions possible.

In all candor, we at Bridgestone Americas never went quite so far, although we probably should have. We did, however, move significantly in that direction. As discussed in the next chapter, we instituted 360-degree reviews for all senior executives, including myself. Both the COO and I, in turn, shared the results of our reviews with the top 150 executives at the semi-annual retreat, along with our commitments to improve our performance. It was not easy to be that vulnerable in front of 150 people. But the team appreciated our transparency and trust skyrocketed through our example.

As important as individual feedback is, it is also important to establish a process where there is a brutally frank discussion with the team after each project to discuss what can be done differently in the future to achieve a better result. This is the well-known concept of continual improvement, also called *kaizen* in Japan. It takes focus to do this on a consistent basis. We were pretty good at engaging in *kaizen* when things didn't go too well.

But we failed to engage in *kaizen* when we believed we did a good job. That was a mistake. As the great Duke basketball coach, Mike Krzyzewski, said, "Winning can cover up poor performance." Moreover, there is always room for improvement, and it would have better sent the message that we strive for excellence in all things.

The bottom line is this: leaders set the standard of acceptable performance – individually and collectively. If they yield on that standard, that then effectively lowers the bar. It is, therefore, a leader's responsibility to set a high standard, and to never yield

---

[7] Ray Dalio, TedTalk, 2017.

on it. As Mac Anderson, founder of Successories and Simple Truths, said, "Quality is the Mother . . . And we don't mess with Mom."[8]

Making the Tough People Decisions and How to Do It

Setting a high standard of performance is meaningful only if, at the end of the day, it has teeth. A leader must commit to acting on their standards. And sometimes that means removing people from the organization.

One common theme I have often heard among CEOs driving change is they regret not removing individuals who didn't align with the future direction, both strategically and culturally, of the organization in a timely manner. These CEOs allowed leaders who didn't align to stick around too long, sometimes for as long as two years. In retrospect, these CEOs said they would give the current leaders no more than six months to champion, in deeds and words, the changes they were trying to make. If they didn't fully get on board, they had to leave.

This action, or perhaps inaction, on dealing with people puts a drag on change. At best, it creates confusion in an organization, as some wonder if the leader is serious about change. At worst, the organization interprets the refusal to deal with resistors as the change effort is not real and won't last. As noted earlier, such a recalcitrant executive, whether their actions are overt or passive aggressive, is a cancer to the organization.

As discussed in the opening of this chapter, we made the tough decision to remove executives who we believed were not a good cultural fit for the organization, even when those individuals obtained excellent results. At times, this was a tsunami for the organization. But it made clear we would act in the most significant ways necessary to achieve our goals. Leaders get what

---

[8] Mac Anderson, *212° Leadership, The 10 Rules for Highly Effective Leadership* (Simple Truths, 2011), 71.

they tolerate. The organization must understand that a leader will take severe action when called for.

The adage goes, "Hire slow, fire fast." Hiring, particularly for certain positions, can be among the most important decisions a leader makes. It must be done carefully. Disney put a senior security executive through 19 interviews before offering him a job. Zappos offers to pay new hires to leave after investing weeks of training in that person, but before they have a chance to poison the organization. We were very careful in our hiring decisions, sometimes frustratingly slow for the candidates. Slow to hire.

The same concept applies to promotions. A leader owes it to all involved, the person being considered for a promotion and that person's family, as well as the team, and the broader organization, to be extremely careful in making such an important decision. This often means moving slowly, deliberately. It may feel good to tell someone they are being promoted, but it feels far worse to tell that person they have failed in their new job, and they are out of work.

"Fire fast" may be an overstatement though. Having hired or promoted someone, we worked hard to give them a reasonable opportunity to succeed – feedback, coaching, etc. That is only fair to them and their families.

But, if that didn't work, we made the tough decision and moved on. Failure to do so keeps an ineffective person in the organization, and others in the organization will believe, rightly so, that performance is not critical to personal success or that management is not serious about what they preach. If management is not doing its job (i.e., getting rid of poor performers and destructive forces in the organization), why should they do theirs. Moreover, if the person is culturally disruptive, regardless of their business success, then others will believe, again rightly so, that management is not serious about culture. And so, the cancer spreads.

As one of my mentors used to say, "It isn't the people you let go who make your job hard, it's the ones you don't."

* * *

When we did let someone go, we did not use them as an example to those who remained. We didn't tell the organization why an individual was being let go. We were affiliative in nature, and compassionate to a fault. If we let someone go, even if they literally robbed the company, we were always gentle in the announcement. We usually explained their departure as a decision on their part to pursue other opportunities. The organization knew exactly what that meant – that is, they were fired – yet the words were never spoken. That was our standard procedure.

Roughly two years after taking over, I discovered that a senior executive was undercutting our cultural changes. The executive was not stealing or engaging in any unethical conduct. It was entirely a cultural issue. The executive was a high-profile member of the team who made significant substantive contributions to the organization. In announcing that person's departure from the company, we put it as gently and compassionately as possible using our standard operating procedure.

This time however, the rumor mill started. Some speculated that the executive must have been fired for disagreeing with me. Such a rumor flew in the face of the courage and candor culture we were trying so hard to create. The rumor was flatly false, however with the lack of information, people have a natural tendency to make up their own version of the story. This time, we knew we had to provide the correct information in order to uphold the values we were creating for our organization.

At a meeting with the senior executive team, we took time to set the record straight, explaining how that individual had been undercutting the culture everyone in the room was working to create. How much easier and more effective would it have been if we had been up front with the organization from the start? If we had explained in the announcement that the person was not advancing the cultural changes we were making, and in some cases had undercut the culture, and therefore the person needed to leave the organization. Details are not necessary in such an announcement, but the true overriding reason usually is. This is not to be cruel, but to be honest. To build trust. When you must make changes don't shy away from explaining why to those that remain. Indeed, it is always better to provide the explanation before there is the accusation. Without information, people sometimes make up their own stories. The truth travels slowly, rumors at the speed of light.

Delegating Properly

Shortly after assuming the CEO role, several of our young and promising executives said in a meeting that we – most executives – needed to do a better job delegating. That is, we needed to delegate more and more often. They were right.

Effective delegation furthers almost every aspect of change. It is likely that no meaningful change in a sizeable team can occur without delegation. Others must share in and drive the vision and the strategy, and help create the processes and policies (alignment) needed for the changes to occur. Moreover, good management requires delegation, both to drive ownership and pride, and to free up the manager to do the things he should be doing. Micromanaging may well be easier, but it is rarely better.

When I first joined Bridgestone's legal department, the new general counsel, my boss, had recently learned of thousands of toxic tort cases against the company. Those are cases where contractors, former employees, and others claimed they were injured by chemicals at our plants. The cases had been assigned to a lawyer whose expertise was in a different area of the law from litigation. The lawyer was hard working, well-intentioned, and knowledgable in his chosen area of expertise. But for these cases he was, in essence, a fish out of water.

And so, the cases were reassigned to me. This freed up the other lawyer to better focus on the things at which he excelled. I, in turn, brought a new perspective to the cases and we were able to resolve them in a manner beneficial to the company.

Delegation can be difficult. Many struggle with letting go of control. It is easier for most to do it themselves. As hard as it is for many to delegate something, it is far more difficult still to effectively delegate a matter or a project. The first consideration in effective delegation is whether the delegatee (as a lawyer would call the person to whom something is being delegated) has the requisite skills and knowledge (or at least has the capability and time to gain the knowledge) for the task.

No one in their right mind would ask me, a lawyer, to perform heart surgery. For that matter, no one would ask their orthopedic surgeon to perform heart surgery, and no orthopedic surgeon would do it even if asked. They simply aren't qualified. So, the first question in any delegation decision is whether the person has the requisite skills and experience to do the job.

If not, do they have the capability (intelligence, humility, mentor, time, etc.) to get those skills in a timely manner?

So, in our example, someone who needs heart surgery obviously goes to a heart surgeon. However, among those surgeons who have the requisite training and experience to perform heart surgery, their skills are certainly not equal. Some are better than others, and that is true in just about everything in life. Some have better tools, better teams working with them, and more experience. Some are more specialized and thus perform certain types of heart surgery but not other types, while other heart surgeons are more generalized. Some are just better than others. For these and other reasons, success rates for heart surgeries vary significantly around the country.

By way of example, I had heart surgery to repair a defective heart valve. The surgery was performed by Dr. Marc Gillinov at the Cleveland Clinic. Why travel all the way to Cleveland for my heart surgery when I don't even live in Ohio? The Cleveland

Clinic's mortality rate for such complicated and delicate surgeries is near zero (certainly a fact that was important to me), and Dr. Gillinov is regarded as among the very best in the world at what he does. And he specializes in certain heart surgeries, including the kind I needed (also very important to me.)

In a follow-up visit some 18 months after the surgery, my local cardiologist (a wonderful man and physician, I might add) praised Dr. Gillinov's work, saying he was "a Leonardo DaVinci and Michelangelo rolled into one," and he questioned whether any other surgeon in the world could have done what he did.

So, before delegating (in this example, asking a surgeon to perform heart surgery), consideration should be given, if circumstances permit, to whom, among all the heart surgeons, is truly at the top of the game for that particular type of surgery. But, of course, this is not limited to heart surgeons or even doctors. Not all lawyers and law firms, teachers, financial advisors, businesspeople, assistants, and so on are equal in their talents, work ethic, judgment, and dedication.

Similarly, no one in their right mind would ask a highly trained heart surgeon to stitch up a small cut on one's arm. That would be overkill.

But, of course, even the very best surgeons had to learn their art. When they started performing such extraordinary surgery, they did so under the tutelage of others. They studied and worked under the watchful eyes and hands of other accomplished surgeons. One of a leader's responsibilities is to develop talent for the future. So, is the matter to be delegated an opportunity for someone to learn? If so, is the person ready to be stretched in this particular assignment? Do they need supervision, and if so, how much supervision? Can you, as the person delegating the assignment, provide that mentorship and, if not, can someone else do that? This is another consideration in the delegation equation.

There is still more. Does that person have the time and the resources needed to do the job effectively? These are obviously important considerations in the delegation equation as well.

Judgment is another extremely important consideration in many delegation decisions. What type of judgment might the situation call for and what kind of judgment does the delegatee (there goes that legal term again) have?

For months, most in the organization continued to act in alignment with the way things used to be and not with the new world we were creating. In our new world, however, we had been tasked with significantly improving the company's financial results. For quite a while some in the organization continued to operate with the old mindset, the old way of doing business. They made decisions that we had to revisit and correct. Some might argue that those people lacked appropriate judgment. I think the issue was different.

They were doing what we had always done. Nothing more and nothing less. It took time for them to learn the new ways we wanted to conduct ourselves. We had to give them time to do this but not too much time. To ensure that they would begin to act consistent with the new culture and new ways we wanted to conduct our business, we had to do something more.

That is, we had to drive alignment throughout the organization. Without alignment of policies, processes, and norms, no change will succeed. It is that critical.

9

Alignment: Lesson #5

"It's not enough to be busy, so are the ants. The question is, what are we busy about?"

— Henry David Thoreau

EIGHT-MAN CREW RACING is exquisite to watch. There is such harmony and synchronization among the team. Each of the eight nearly 12-foot-long oars seemingly enter and leave the water at the same moment, as if the result of a fine-timed Swiss watch. This is no accident. It is essential if the team wants to win. Tiny differences in timing or oar pressure can disrupt the optimal flow of the boat, causing it to yaw or wobble, which in turn results in drag, and drag in turn reduces speed. Even small fluctuations among the oars, or uneven pressure of the oars as they are pulled through the water, can mean the difference between winning and losing, qualifying for the Olympics or watching others compete from the sidelines. If a team works harder and better, not as individuals but as a team, if they have outstanding alignment, the team has a fighting chance to win. Without it, they will pack their bags and go home.

Certainly, in the tire business as in many other businesses, alignment is critical for success. Each tire factory makes hundreds if not thousands of different tires. Many tire types are produced in many different sizes. Depending on the degree of size variation within a given tire, the actual construction of it might change to handle different vehicle weights or performance objectives. A tire factory also produces similar but different tires that focus more on one characteristic, such as mileage versus performance. And many factories also produce several different tire types such as snow tires, ultra-high-performance tires, and so on.

For some tires, the demand is in the millions, while for others it may be only 10,000 per year. So, a tire company must do a good job calculating the demand for its tires, not just in macro numbers, but also down to the individual SKU micro level. Among other things, this requires purchasing the different raw materials and producing the many components, all in the right quantities, for each of the many different tire types and SKUs in each factory that makes those tires and having the materials and components available in the factory at the right time.

Then, of course, some tires, both by size and type, sell more in some regions and less in others. An obvious example is tire companies don't sell many snow tires in Florida. But there are countless other non-obvious examples based on the preferences and driving patterns across the United States, much less other parts of the world. Making the right tire at the right time, and then having that tire in the right warehouse and distribution center, requires extraordinary alignment.

The need for alignment is not limited to the ordinary conduct of the business. It is equally essential to driving change successfully. If some are driving the change and others are resisting or even pushing change in a different direction, the change will not succeed. Change, in turn, is essential for long-term viability. As leaders attempt to change a team's direction, or a division or company's strategy, focus, or culture, it is imperative that there be complete alignment throughout the team and the organization. Without alignment, there is little or no chance the change will work.

A wonderful example of alignment is Starbucks. The former head of marketing of Starbucks spoke at one of the company's events, and he shared a big part of Starbucks' success. When the coffee shop company was a fraction of its current size, a small team of people within the company concluded that its strategy was to be the "Third Place." For most people there is "home," and home often means chores to be done, kids to take care of, and much stress. Then (especially prior to the COVID pandemic) there is "work," again a place of stress. Starbucks was to be the "Third Place," a place where anyone could go to have a good cup of coffee, relax, and stay as long as they wanted to escape all the stresses of the other places in their life.

For this strategy to work, everything had to be aligned with the concept of being the "Third Place." The chairs and couches and colors had to be inviting and relaxing, almost homey; the smells had to be dominated by the aroma of coffee, thus, even in China where smoking is not prohibited indoors, it is nonetheless prohibited in Starbucks; the music had to be at just the right volume and type, softer and mellower in the morning than in the afternoon. Every detail, from how baristas greeted customers to the lighting and Wi-Fi service, had to support the "Third-Place" environment. The company even consciously decided that the extra cost of having double ply toilet paper was one of the many requirements for the stores to truly be the "Third Place." The strategy worked, in large part because the company completely aligned with the concept of the "Third Place." Starbucks grew to its extraordinary worldwide presence today.

That is alignment and it is essential for change and success.

* * *

Alignment means consistency and support among all policies, processes, structure, and strategies that, in any way, influence conduct or the change that the leader seeks. HR policies and processes, for example, often influence behavior as do many finance policies. If a company attempts to instill outstanding customer service yet does not give latitude to employees and managers to make customers happy because that could cost money, that is a lack of alignment. The company might talk the talk about customer service, but significant limitations on customer concessions says the opposite.

Alignment is similar to, but different from focused execution, which is discussed in the next chapter. Yet, both are critical to change, and they do indeed overlap much like a Venn diagram. Alignment ensures that both the organizational structure and entire collection of policies and processes support rather than thwart the desired end. Focused execution is the intense, unyielding, relentless determination to see that the goals are accomplished. Alignment puts the foundation in place and focused execution brings it to life. Again, if the goal is outstanding customer service, alignment is creating the policies and processes that allow such customer service to be a reality. When an individual within the company doesn't quite get it or do it for whatever reason, focused execution means identifying and working with that individual to help them change their behavior or removing that individual if that is what it takes to reach the overriding vision.

Alignment is part of the hard work of change. Setting the vision is the fun, easier part, although not without its challenges. Executives typically go off site to plan and strategize. A consultant may be hired to help develop the future direction of the company. The hard work comes with actually creating all the new policies, processes, structure, and strategies needed to make that future direction become a reality.

In his book *Built to Last*, Jim Collins discovered that great companies, companies that have lasted more than 100 years, all had clear visions. After the book was published, this became the fad in the business world. Yet, most companies, including those that do not stand the test of time, created visions. But their visions became little more than words hung on a conference room wall. When employees were interviewed about the vision or the values of an organization, the interviewer would most likely get a sarcastic response like, "Ha, seriously, that is just what they say. That is not really how things are done around here." There was, to be short, lack of alignment and also focused execution.

So, once the vision is set and the culture defined or redefined, the entire organization must be aligned to achieve them. This is critical for lasting change to become a reality and true transformation to take place.

* * *

We wanted to drive greater innovation at Bridgestone Americas. It needed to become our mantra and our focus. This required ensuring that we were making products that met the spoken and unspoken wants and needs of the Boss (the end-user). It also meant having a culture dominated by courage and candor and inclusiveness. For each of these and so many other changes, it required realigning the organization.

To bring Bridgestone Americas into alignment around the new vision and culture, we had to, among other things, create an innovation structure and process.

To that end, I asked the COO to lead a committee to both formalize this process and drive the spirit and acts of innovation throughout the organization. His committee created what we called the Bridgestone Innovation Gateway, an online tool to help drive innovation. It allowed thousands of people throughout the organization to submit innovation ideas to an innovation team.

The innovation team was a group comprised of several of our most promising and talented junior executives, which proved to be an invaluable experience for them. One brilliant and enthusiastic young lady was selected to head up the team, and she reported directly to the COO. She then selected others to fill out the innovation group. That group worked closely with me and the COO as well as other members of the senior executive team.

Totally apart from the excellent work they did, it was another way to provide a great employee experience as we pursued being a premier place to work, the third pillar.

The innovation team selected the most interesting ideas and periodically presented them to senior management. Senior management then selected those ideas it believed were worth investing in, and a small team was created and charged with bringing the idea to fruition. That team reported regularly to senior management, as senior management owns the future of the company.

Not infrequently, an innovation team created to pursue an idea would conclude, for one reason or another, that the idea just couldn't work. That was okay. Usually, the problem was because of some internal roadblock or a technology limitation. In the former case, senior management removed the roadblock. In the latter case, senior management either agreed and the project ended, and the team was thanked for their excellent work, or, if senior management disagreed, we explained that more work needed to be done to try to overcome the technology roadblock.

There was an added benefit to this process. Those individuals working on an innovation project had regular and meaningful interaction with senior management. It was a tremendous learning experience for them, and it gave us further insight into our high-potential talent.

We also held innovation contests where everyone in the organization was invited to submit an innovation idea. The innovation team selected the finalists who then presented their ideas to senior management.

One of the many ideas that came out of the Bridgestone Innovation Gateway was a mobile tire installation service. The idea was that someone could either call or order tires online and, rather than going into a store to have the tires installed, we would go to them. A specially designed and equipped van would meet the customer at the place and time of their choosing – their home or work, for example – and install the new tires on their car. So, a stay-at-home mom would not have to worry about taking her kids to a tire store to get new tires. A doctor would not have to leave his practice when his tires wore out. It was all about making tire buying easier for the Boss. It was simple, logical, and brilliant.

Those customers who used what ultimately became known as Firestone Direct uniformly raved about it. It made tire buying convenient and easy in our fast-paced, stressful world. Today, Firestone Direct has expanded to offer oil changes and other services. But this all came about through our attempts to drive a culture of innovation and focus on the Boss.

The point is that being innovative was not just talked about, but a structured innovation process was created and rolled out to the entire organization. That is alignment. It took time, effort, and money, but it was unquestionably worth the investment.

Indeed, the impact of driving innovation on the organization's culture was profound. People within the organization knew that we were serious about the new focus on innovation and the Boss, and, most importantly, they were energized and engaged by it. They recognized they could make a difference not only in their assigned responsibilities, but by contributing ideas that could have a meaningful impact on our business. As we said again and again, good ideas can come from anywhere.

The efforts to drive innovation spread throughout the company. The tire development and research group created an innovation lab where engineers and scientists could explore new and often exciting technological possibilities. The tire development team used their imagination and began developing an extraordinary list of potential innovations to help the Boss. The tire engineers, chemists, and other scientists in the Tire Development and Research teams were energized by the opportunities for innovation. Their enthusiasm showed when they presented their ideas to senior management; they were the proverbial kid in a candy store.

Firestone Industrial Products, one of Bridgestone Americas non-tire businesses, started holding special events for the entire business to showcase their innovation ideas and product prototypes that were developed under the company's new vision and culture. Not only were their engineers invigorated, but the entire organization was excited about the future. One of their new, innovative products was selected by a leading electric car innovator and manufacturer.

Firestone Fibers and Textiles developed a new material that had the promise of greatly improving bulletproof vests. Firestone Building Products created a new marketing tool to help customers better understand their products and decide which would be best for them. The innovation spirit was overwhelming.

The effects went beyond Bridgestone Americas. As Bridgestone in Japan learned of our innovation and cultural initiatives, it developed its own global innovation contests, and the concept of the Bridgestone Innovation Gateway spread throughout the broader organization. The energy was simply tremendous as was the cultural impact.

At the end of the day, it is one thing to talk about innovation being important. But talk is cheap. The tools and processes to drive innovation had to be created and become part of the business. Without that alignment, we unquestionably would have reverted to our previous ways. Innovation would have only been talk. Bridgestone Americas was not only talking the talk but walking the walk.

* * *

To ensure that the Rules of the Road came alive, however, we had to do more than create a formal innovation process. The performance review processes had to be changed, too. Specifically, leaders had to be held accountable to drive the Rules of the Road, Bridgestone Americas cultural blueprint, into our daily thinking and behaviors. Moreover, leaders and managers had to actually live the Rules of the Road.

A few months after adopting the Rules of the Road, the Executive Committee decided that going forward 55 percent of an individual's performance would be based on meeting performance objectives and 45 percent on living the Rules of the Road. The split could well have been 50-50, but 55-45 conveyed the message of the importance of meeting the company's financial and business commitments. Giving a 45 percent emphasis on how a person behaves meant achieving our financial and business goals had to be done a certain way, with a certain acceptable leadership style. Without living the Rules of the Road, an individual could not possibly receive a satisfactory much less outstanding performance review, regardless of their business accomplishments.

To overhaul the performance review process, the HR team created a process and structure so that supporting the Rules of the Road would be based on hard data, rather than just a supervisor's perceptions. Each of the top 150 leaders in the company had an annual 360 review and those reviews were designed to parrot the Rules of the Road. An individual's direct reports, colleagues, and supervisor were all anonymously surveyed (and, to avoid cherry picking, their manager had to agree which colleagues were included in the survey), and those tallies largely determined if an individual was living and advancing the company's cultural objectives.

This hard data provided strong evidence that a leader either was or was not sufficiently advancing the new culture. The individual could not reasonably disagree with the hard facts of how others observed his or her behaviors. It was powerful.

The COO and I were included in this process as well. We shared the results of our reviews with the top 150 people in the company at the semi-annual off-site meeting, and we made commitments to that team on what steps we would take to improve our cultural performance. This was scary, but by being part of the process rather than apart from it, the entire program had enormous credibility. It concretely showed that we were serious about the culture at every level, and we were determined for it to become the norm within the company. We aligned our processes with the culture we sought to create.

* * *

Another example of aligning Bridgestone Americas' processes with meeting the wants and needs of the Boss was the creation of a new workflow for new tire development. Under the old process, sales or marketing would usually take what they had heard from our tire dealers and ask for a new product that would fill a gap in our offerings, such as a slick looking new SUV tire. We did not, however, have data from the Boss to either support or refine those perceptions and, most importantly, to define that new tire's most important performance characteristics.

We wanted the process to be more data driven. The Product, Development, and Research Committee created under the governance process discussed in the leadership chapter requested that our new chief marketing officer work with the different parts of the organization and design a new tire development process. The hallmarks of the process that team created was that it started with intensive research on what the Boss expected for each particular type of tire. Based on that data, the marketing group would set the key performance characteristics for the tire in question. Of course, if the tire development team determined a performance characteristic was technologically unachievable, the parameters would then be revised with marketing's agreement. Performance gates and check points were developed to ensure that the tire being developed was, in fact, the tire that was requested.

The process did not end there. Once a tire was introduced into the marketplace, marketing would follow Boss feedback and other hard data they collected to ensure that the tire was indeed performing as intended. Occasionally, a tire would perform differently in the extraordinary and varied environments and stresses of the real world versus the testing facility and the lab. If a tire was falling short of the Boss's expectations, then the tire design group would tweak the design to get it right.

All of this was done to ensure complete alignment with the first Rule of the Road – the Boss is #1.

* * *

Alignment is critical for successful change, and it is the change leader's responsibility to ensure that all policies, processes, structures, and strategies align with the goals. Where they do not, the leader must task (delegate) the appropriate people and groups to make the necessary changes. This is part of leadership.

We started every Bridgestone Americas town hall meeting with a presentation to update the organization on the progress of achieving our vision and the Four Pillars. With the addition of innovation as the foundation to everything we do, we added a section on innovation to our town hall meetings. This reinforcement helped align the entire organization around our vision, the Four Pillars (our strategic goals), and the Rules of the Road. Our semi-annual off-site meetings, our innovation processes, our tire development process, our performance reviews, our people changes, and so much more were all efforts to align our large and diverse group of employees around our common vision and cultural blueprint so that we were all rowing in the same direction.

Failure to drive alignment is no different than failing to walk the walk. The leader says one thing, but the policies and processes tell a very different story to the team. The lack of alignment reveals the stark reality that management is either not serious or, worse, disingenuous. In such cases, the results will satisfy very few.

Alignment takes a lot of hard work by many people. But it is essential if the changes are to come to fruition. Total complete alignment in every policy, process, and strategy. No detail can be left untouched. Total commitment to the goal, just as Starbucks did with the colors, sounds, smells, and even the toilet paper to create the "Third Place." Just as Bridgestone Americas did with its innovation process, HR programs, and tire development process. All in, all the time. Perfect synchronization, like a world-class crew team.

10

Focused Execution: Lesson #6

"Strategy is important, but execution is everything."

– Jeff Haden

THE ORIGINAL EQUIPMENT (OE) team within Bridgestone Americas was responsible for tire sales to what had long been called original equipment customers – General Motors, Toyota, and other car manufacturers. It was called this because the tires sold to them were installed as "original equipment" on the car as opposed to replacement tires that the car owner buys from a tire retailer when the original tires that came on the car need to be replaced. Bridgestone Americas sold millions of tires every year to car companies, and it was a critical part of the business. Among other things, it kept the factories running and greatly lowered the cost per tire as the fixed costs were spread over a greater number of units. The tire factories alone represent a very large, fixed cost.

In part due to their huge buying power, car companies are superb at beating down the price from their suppliers. This certainly is the case in the tire industry. Moreover, when a company agreed to sell tires to a car company, the price was set for years. If raw material or other costs, such as transportation costs to ship the tires, went up, that would further eat into the tire company's profits. But, often times, when the car owner needs to replace the original tires on their vehicle, they would do so with the same type of tires that were on the car, and the tire company would get a more reasonable return at that point.

Further, the car companies' high standards for both quality and tire characteristics helped force Bridgestone to maintain excellent manufacturing standards and cutting-edge technologies.[1] It was also prestigious for the brand to be on high-end cars such as a Cadillac, BMW, and Lexus. For all these reasons, most major tire manufacturers sell tires to car companies.

If Bridgestone Americas was going to significantly improve our financial results, we had to start earning a more reasonable profit in our OE business. For the reasons discussed above, this was easier said than done.

The OE team, like most businesses, sought to grow its business. Early in our change strategy, we informed the team that they could not increase their volume of sales beyond specified amounts until their profits improved by an agreed upon amount. This restriction on their business was discouraging to the team. It did, however, send the message that we were serious about improving profits. That, in turn, drove the OE team to be more aggressive in negotiations over the price of tires.

After several discussions, we also informed the team that from that point forward our contracts to sell tires to car companies

---

[1] I have heard the belief that tire companies sell cheap, low-quality tires to car companies, and that is why some OE tires do not last 40,000 miles plus. This is flatly wrong, at least in my experience. The tires sold to car companies, at least by Bridgestone, were of extraordinary and exacting quality. The reason why some of those tires might not last as long as some car owners preferred was that the tires were designed with different performance characteristics such as superb handling, which can negatively impact how long a tire lasts. By way of example, an IndyCar racing tire has phenomenal stopping and cornering ability. But to achieve that level of performance, those tires need to be replaced after roughly 80 miles or so. In any event, those performance characteristics are established by the car companies.

must have a raw material adjustment clause. That clause would, in effect, raise the price of tires as raw material costs increased. Understandably, the car companies demanded that the raw material adjustment clause provide that the price of our tires would lower if raw material costs went down. That was fine with us, as we were not trying to gouge our important customers, but only protect a reasonable profit for our business.

After a few years, the OE team's profit picture improved significantly, and it stayed that way. It became a good and reliable business division, and a significant reason for the overall improvements in Bridgestone America's financial statements. But it would not have happened without intense focus and execution by all involved.

The focus on improving the OE business went further still. We had to find a way to develop tires for car manufacturers that the consumer – the purchaser of the vehicle and who we now called the Boss – was happy with, so a greater percent would purchase Bridgestone (or Firestone, as the case may be) replacement tires when the time came. To do this, the marketing team conducted extensive research by car and tire type to discover the key characteristics that consumers wanted in their tires. One of those characteristics was mileage. The research revealed that consumer mileage expectations differed for different types of tires on different types of vehicles. So, we established internal mileage standards that our OE tires had to meet by vehicle type.

The challenge was that we couldn't just impose those standards without the car manufacturer's consent. The team worked with our car company customers, sharing the data, helping to convince them that these minimum mileage standards were, ultimately, in both Bridgestone's and the car manufacturer's best interests. It was hard work. It did not happen overnight. It took many months. Yet, most car companies agreed. And it resulted in a win for us, a win for the car manufacturer, and, importantly, a win for the Boss.

Through all this hard work by many people, the OE part of the business became even more valuable to the business. But the bigger point is this: without intense focus, persistence, and determination, habits or processes simply will not change. Sometimes that focus can come from the head of the team, department, or division, and other times it must come from the head of the organization.

Make no mistake, that focus, what I call *focused execution*— the sixth and final requirement for change—is critical for meaningful change to stick. In its absence, the desired change will so often fall by the wayside. The resistance to change, the ingrained habits, or the simple lack of energy will prevail over the momentum and drive needed to successfully implement change. For meaningful change to happen, focused execution must be the order of the day every day. Like the prior five requirements of change, without it, change will not happen.

* * *

There is an outstanding book called *Lessons from Private Equity Every Company Can Use*.[2] The book's premise is straightforward. Successful private equity firms are extremely good at what they do: turning around a company in relatively short order and then reaping the rewards by selling it at a substantial profit. The book explains how private equity performs these turnaround miracles and argues other companies can use the same techniques to improve their business. One of the tools described in the book is intense and unyielding focus on those key items that must change for the company to improve. It is that kind of focus that drives change, and in its absence, change is likely to succumb to the resistors of change or the habits and ease of doing things the way they were always done.

Thomas Edison was certainly one of the greatest inventors of all time. He had a staggering 1,093 US patents, including the light bulb, movie camera, phonograph, alkaline battery, and even

---

[2] Orit Gadiesh and Hugh MacArthur, *Lessons from Private Equity Any Company Can Use* (Harvard Business Press, 2008).

an electric voting machine. Edison is reported to have said, "Genius is 1 percent inspiration and 99 percent hard work."[3] Edison failed a thousand times before succeeding in his efforts to invent the first light bulb. Although Edison himself would say that he never failed. He learned a thousand different ways how NOT to make a light bulb. Nevertheless, he had a Vision, and the determination, the persistence, and the focus to achieve his Vision. Without that focus, someone else likely would have created the first electric light bulb.

The same is said to be true of Bill Gates. He had an extraordinary "ability to dream big and pursue that with single-minded determination."[4] It is hard to imagine that Steve Jobs, Jeff Bezos, Elon Musk, or other hugely successful, innovative people would have enjoyed their success without extraordinary focus. Focused execution is required to effect change.

* * *

Changing Bridgestone Americas' culture was one of the most important and challenging of all the changes made during my tenure as CEO. It would not have happened just by introducing the concept of innovation as a cultural change agent. To happen, it required follow through – both alignment and focused execution. New innovation processes as well as living the new culture became an integral part of every leader and manager's goals.

The concept of innovation and the Rules of the Road were created at the first off-site meeting with the top 150 executives in the company. For the next several years, most of the subsequent semi-annual off-site meetings with that group continued to focus on developing leadership skills and behaviors that drove the culture we desired until the changes had taken sufficient root that we could move on to other issues.

---

[3] WikiQuotes.
[4] B V Krishnamurthy, "Bill Gates: Entrepreneur, Manager, and Leader," *Harvard Business Review*, June 27, 2008.

Before one of these off-site meetings, HR worked with a management consulting firm to conduct a 180-degree assessment of each of the top 150 leaders who were to attend the meeting. By surveying those people who both reported directly to and frequently worked with each leader, the assessments identified each individual's predominate leadership style and the "climate" they created as leaders because of that leadership style. At the off-site meeting, the consultant provided a detailed assessment of the prevailing leadership styles within Bridgestone Americas taken as a whole.

Some of our leaders were using command and control (top-down decision-making) and pace-setting (micromanagement) more than they probably should have. Being told what to do and how to do it tends to stifle ideas and initiative.

The consultant then conducted a workshop on how we could improve our styles so that we could become more collaborative, do a better job creating an environment for debate and discussion, and one in which leaders set the direction and then delegated appropriately. At the end of the meeting, each of the top 150 leaders received the results of their individual leadership assessment, and we offered outside coaching at the company's expense to each for their improvement journey.

For the leadership meeting six months later, we hired an organization out of New York that interviewed over 40 of our executives. They then put on a series of vignettes mimicking what they had been told in the interviews about Bridgestone Americas' internal behaviors and the way leaders interact with each other and subordinates. Of course, the names of the characters in the vignettes were completely fictional, as the goal was not to embarrass anyone. Rather, the exercise was intended to hold up a mirror to ourselves.

Following each vignette, the consultants led a series of discussions about the behaviors. The mirror showed we still had a lot of work to do, but it also showed we were making progress. To say it was powerful is an understatement.

As these new skills were developed and ingrained over the next few years, our leaders turned into teachers. We rolled out a program called Creating a Culture of Innovation. This program, along with the innovation and HR review processes that were now built into the organization, not only showed Bridgestone Americas was serious about the new culture, but it helped make the new culture come alive.

Once the foundation was laid, our direction set, and our leaders aligned, the semi-annual leadership meetings focused on developing and executing the new skills, tools, and processes to accomplish our vision. The meetings shifted focus to things like eliminating inherent bias to help ensure effective decision-making and improving our cash conversion cycle. But even as we moved on to such matters, as important as they were, portions of the meetings continued to focus on driving the new culture. This was part of our focused execution to drive the Rules of the Road into the DNA of Bridgestone Americas' culture.

* * *

It certainly took considerably more than these off-site meetings to drive the Rules of the Road. We aligned our performance review process to the Rules of the Road, and it took continued focus to make them come alive. While most executives did a very good job adopting the new culture, for others it took more work and time to fully "get it." We provided coaching and we had frank discussions with teammates who struggled with the new culture. We made it clear, however that the Rules of the Road were nonnegotiable.

There were, unfortunately, some who just couldn't or wouldn't make the adjustment. Several of these individuals were exceptionally talented and brought considerable strengths to the table in their respective areas of expertise. Some were friends. We hated to lose their talents, but we either walked the walk or the whole cultural change effort would fall apart. We could not make exceptions, regardless of the friendship or skills they offered. If they didn't perform according to Bridgestone Americas' values, the Rules of the Road, then they were not performing. One exception, one crack in the dike, and the entirety of everyone's efforts would have been at risk. That is all part of focused execution.

As one CEO put it, if you don't understand the new culture, I have all day to help explain it to you. But if you won't adopt the new culture, once understood, then we must part ways.

* * *

To help drive the culture through the ranks, I also held monthly lunches with about 10 people who in the ordinary course of business would have no personal interaction with senior management. The individuals were picked randomly, and they were encouraged in the 90-minute luncheon meeting to share any thoughts and concerns and ask any questions that they had about the organization and the business. I also often held these lunches when I traveled to various company offices for meetings. It's worth noting that other members of senior management were not invited to these lunches so the participants could speak as freely as possible.

The main purposes of these luncheons were to be transparent, learn what people were thinking, and to let others throughout the organization know that courage and candor meant they could ask the CEO anything. They could express any concerns they had, and I would do my best to understand their concerns. answer questions, and address issues as appropriate. It also helped show that we were open to the ideas of others throughout the organization because good ideas can come from anywhere. A senior member of our HR team planned these lunches and encouraged the attendees to come prepared with questions and comments. She helped alleviate some of the fear or trepidations one might have when joining the CEO for lunch.

The top executives and I each worked hard to make certain that in all meetings, others were free to voice their opinion and argue their case. We religiously insisted that all the right people had to be at the table before making a decision, both so we could make the best decision possible and so the right hand knew what the left hand was doing.

I almost always surveyed meeting participants for their opinions before voicing my own. The participants might have different perspectives that could change my mind on a given issue, and if they went first, they weren't swayed by what I might be thinking. They couldn't, in effect, cater to my views.

The benefit of this was exemplified in one extremely important meeting. For over a year we had been working on a new and potentially industry-altering project with a third party. It was truly innovative, but it also had significant risks.

We were at a crossroad; we had to decide whether to proceed with the transaction or scrap the proposition.

I went around the room asking each person whether they thought we should proceed with the transaction, and why or why not. I deliberately started with the more junior people in the room so I could hear their perspectives before the senior people piped in and influenced them. Person after person reviewed the pros and cons as they saw it, said the decision was a close call, and on balance they thought we should proceed with the transaction.

I then asked the general counsel, an extremely bright and capable individual, for his opinion. In the face of the businesspeople he counseled and worked with day in and day out, and whose trust he constantly strived to maintain, he courageously gave a cogent explanation why, from a business standpoint (as opposed to a legal standpoint) we should not proceed with the transaction. Nor did he know my and the COO's thoughts on whether we should proceed with the transaction. Even though the businesspeople in the room said we should proceed with the deal, the general counsel, with courage and candor, disagreed, and explained why.

It was a great moment for the company. The courage and candor we had been working so hard to achieve was taking place.

Both the COO and I agreed with him, and the company took a different path than the transaction under consideration, which, in the fullness of time, proved to be the right decision.

But to get the executive team to a point where those kinds of intense debates occurred took determination, patience, and focus. The benefits, however, were enormous, both for the substantive results and the engagement of the team.

* * *

Focused execution is similar to, but different from, alignment, which pertains to the procedures, policies, and strategies. Focused execution, rather, makes the changes a reality; it is the follow-up on those policies and processes, the decisions that are made, to ensure that the vision and goals are achieved. It requires an unrelenting determination to see the changes through.

The whole of a leader's words and actions, the majority of their time and efforts, must be to drive the needed changes. This includes making certain all team members are on board and doing their share. When they can't or won't, the leader must act. It is making sure the policies and procedures work as intended, that the behaviors and decisions drive the end goals, keeping in mind, "stubborn on the vision, flexible on the details." Focused execution, at the end of the day, drives the sought-after results.

11

Restoring an Iconic Brand with the Six Lessons

THE FIRESTONE BRAND was significantly damaged by the Ford–Firestone tire recall in 2000. The company recalled millions of Firestone tires amidst the claim that they caused hundreds of deaths. Ford then removed millions more Firestone tires from its vehicles as part of its battle with us over who was to blame.

As a result of the recall and the damage to the Firestone name, another car company insisted that the Firestone brand tires we sold to them be replaced with Bridgestone brand tires. Consumers were leery of Firestone tires as well. Sales of the once popular tire brand plummeted. And while the company never jettisoned the Firestone brand, it understandably focused on building the highly regarded, yet at the time the lesser known, Bridgestone brand. Thus, much of our advertising budget and sales efforts went to promote Bridgestone tires.

It worked. Bridgestone brand recognition improved significantly and became stronger than ever in North America. Our tire dealers still wanted Firestone tires, however, as they very much saw a place for the brand in their offerings. Many consumers, over time, also wanted the iconic tires. Moreover, some dealers were essentially inseparable from Firestone. It was in their business name, like Bob's Firestone. The Firestone name also was inseparable from our Firestone Complete Auto Care nationwide network of stores.

For this and other reasons, some 10 years after the recall, I was strongly of the opinion that Bridgestone Americas needed to rebuild the Firestone brand. The story of rebuilding the brand was a huge success, and a microcosm of the importance of each of the six lessons to successfully driving change.

The first morning our new chief marketing officer (CMO) joined the company, I tasked him with rebuilding the Firestone brand. Of course, this was discussed previously in the interview process.

His first step was to build a world-class marketing team. He made a number of excellent hires, and he also retained the renowned advertising agency Leo Burnett to assist in developing a campaign to rebuild the Firestone brand. He kept me and the COO informed of his progress, which culminated in a meeting in Indianapolis, two days before the running of the Indianapolis 500. It was an appropriate setting as all Indy race cars utilize Firestone tires, and over its 100-year history more cars had won the Indy 500 with Firestone tires than any other tire brand.

The meeting began with a review of the history and current use of the Firestone brand. Firestone continued to be a well-recognized tire brand, and most of the company's roughly 2,200 retail automotive and tire stores across the country were named Firestone Complete Auto Care. Yet, one of the issues, which the company had never completely addressed, was how to effectively market both Firestone tires and the Firestone stores at the same time and in a synergistic way.

The team then took a deep dive into the different segments of the consumer tire market, and the team made the case that the Firestone brand had unique appeal to hard-working people who cherished their cars, pickup trucks, and SUVs. This included those who collect and restore cars as well as all consumers who consider their car a treasured possession. Moreover, positioning the brand this way was consistent with the brand's history, and resonated for the positioning of both the tires themselves as well as our stores. It also drew a distinction between Firestone and Bridgestone, which was our high-technology, cutting-edge brand, and for consumers who drove luxury vehicles.

The CMO and his team detailed their vision for a series of television ads reintroducing the Firestone brand, some that were primarily about the tires and others that were primarily about the stores. The look, feel and messages for the various ads would be the similar. They also walked through the vision for how the stores themselves should look and feel, including the in-store ad campaigns, how the stores should treat and interact with their customers, and how the stores should back up the message with the service they delivered. All of it would be consistent with the same messaging: targeting hard-working people who loved their cars. Firestone, they said, should further tie itself to the growing country music fan base.

At the conclusion of the presentation, one executive in the room jokingly commented that his only concern was that the campaign was so compelling that we might not ever sell another Bridgestone tire.

The campaign, which is still being used today, is "Drive a Firestone." A country music singer with an incredible baritone voice, Trace Adkins, did the voice-over for most of the ads. His deep and sincere intonations could not have been more perfect.

The campaign was a huge success. One of our thematic ads was nominated for a Clio, the premiere award for the advertising industry. The stores, employees, and dealers loved it. The company-owned Firestone stores made all the requisite changes to deliver on the high-quality service message conveyed in the ads. For the first time since Bridgestone and Firestone merged in 1988, there was a marketing campaign that drew a distinction between the two brands and brought Firestone tires and stores under one unifying umbrella.

Most importantly, the consuming public loved it as well. Firestone brand recognition grew to heights it hadn't experienced for years.

The Firestone brand required compelling change if we were to get full value out of it. This change was the product of each of the six requirements to change. It took both leadership (building trust with the propensity and courage to act) and vision (what the world could be) to decide to invest in rebuilding the Firestone brand and to develop a compelling campaign that unified both Firestone tires and Firestone stores. That was no small decision as it was a commitment of a substantial amount of human and financial resources.

Our newfound culture allowed us – no, required us – to focus on the Boss to understand what about Firestone would resonate with them. Further, the culture mandated that all the relevant parts of the organization be involved in developing the campaign. That included marketing, sales, and the company-owned stores, among others. Different parts of the organization were working together to an extraordinary degree.

We had built the right team, the right people, both inside and outside the company to develop and effectuate this campaign. They made all the difference. They conceived and developed a company-wide, comprehensive campaign based on market data that resonated with all stakeholders. We provided the necessary resources and empowered the team to develop an extraordinary campaign to revitalize the iconic Firestone brand.

We had complete alignment with our company-owned stores, and other relevant parts of the organization fully embraced the campaign – from ensuring that the service quality matched the promise of the Drive a Firestone message to embracing the look and feel of the message throughout the store operations. And it took enormous focused execution by the entire team to develop and successfully implement the campaign, and then live the promise the campaign messaged to the consumer – the Boss.

They kept their foot on the pedal throughout, and the dream became a reality.

This campaign was indeed a microcosm of the six lessons for change.

* * *

We, the entire management team, made enormous changes at Bridgestone Americas. Everything was in play. But make no mistake, without the efforts of the entire leadership team and many others throughout the organization, this book would never have been written, because we would not have had the success that we did.

During my tenure as CEO, change was the order of the day. Everything was in play. Profits grew fivefold in six years, achieving a record each year. Our profit performance outperformed the S&P 500 over that same period. With our growth in revenues and profits, Bridgestone became the largest tire and rubber company in the world. Our cash flow improved dramatically, and our debt was reduced enormously. This allowed us to invest in our people, our manufacturing capacity, and our brands. And all of this was achieved through organic changes, that is, without the potential benefits that a large acquisition can sometimes bring.

Our record results demonstrated that when the six lessons for change are implemented, not just preached, very good things can happen. Great success can occur.

* * *

We live in an ever-changing world. Technology, consumer preferences, climate change, pandemics, and many other external and internal factors will force businesses to change their strategies, products, services, culture, and the way they do business in the years to come. Some will be blind to the need for change altogether. Others will attempt changes but fail, and be a part of the roughly 70 percent of change efforts that fall well short of the mark. Others still will use the six lessons of change, successfully implement the needed changes, and take their business or groups to new heights. That is the role of leaders.

Acknowledgments

I OWE MANY people a great deal of thanks. First, the success I had as the CEO of Bridgestone Americas would not have been possible without a true team effort. Included among those, but by no means is this everyone, are Bill Thompson, Phillip Dobbs, TJ Higgins, Stu Crum, Jan Steinmetz, Chris Nicastro, John Baratta, Kurt Danielson, Tim Walsh, Chris Karbowiak, Paul Oakley, Jason Fisher, Saul Solomon, Mike Kane, Michele Herlein, Larry MaGee, Duke Nishiyama, Mick Suzuki, and Tak Sasaki. To each of you, the enormous changes we made together and the success we had were made possible by your hard work, great character, and willingness to believe in our joint vision.

A special debt of gratitude is owed to Bridgestone Americas' chief operating officer from 2010 to 2013, Eduardo Minardi, as well as the person who replaced him when Eduardo was appointed to head Bridgestone Europe and who ultimately succeeded me as the CEO of Bridgestone Americas, Gordon Knapp. Your wise counsel and agenda-free partnership with me was invaluable, and none of this would have happened without you.

Moreover, the extraordinary opportunity given to me to lead Bridgestone Americas is due to the trust and insight of Shoshi Arakawa, the global Bridgestone CEO. Mr. Arakawa took a substantial risk in asking the then general counsel to lead the transformation of Bridgestone Americas. Thank you for believing in me. Mr. Arakawa then showed remarkable leadership and even greater trust by giving me and my COO complete license in how to transform the organization. Your remarkable trust and foresight were rewarded with record profits every year of my tenure.

I have had numerous mentors along my journey, people from whom I have learned an enormous amount about my profession, business, and leadership, and without whom any professional success I have had would have been far less. I hesitate to name any of them for fear of inadvertently excluding someone, but nonetheless, great thanks to Colin Smith, Tom Gardner (a very dear friend and mentor who passed away several years ago and who I miss to this day), Aubrey Harwell, Don Groninger, Dave Thomas, and Hal Horton. Additionally, Oscar Rivera and Jeff Kirschner, both formerly of the Hay Group, and Felix Stellmaszek and Joerg Matthiessen, both of the Boston Consulting Group, could not have been of greater assistance than they were at various times during my tenure as CEO. An additional profound debt is owed to Evelyn Frye.

A particularly special and profound debt of gratitude is owed to my very dear friend and mentor, who also is an outstanding lawyer and man, Jim Karen. He pushed and inspired me in many ways through the years, far more than he knows, and he took the time to review two drafts of this manuscript. His deep and thoughtful review and comments turned this book into something I am proud of.

Another very dear friend, Dan Moore, is a leader and person for whom I have enormous respect. He helped Bridgestone Americas' store network raise their game to the next level and he also took time out of his extremely busy schedule to review a manuscript of this book and provided me with reassurance that the book is worthy of publication.

I would be greatly remiss if I did not acknowledge the outstanding work of Julie Kerr, who provided countless editorial comments on the manuscripts. She not only was a delight to work with but made the final product far better than it would have been without her great work. I also greatly appreciate the assistance of Michele Herlein, who made several significant contributions to the book.

My parents and grandparents each taught me invaluable lessons about myself, others, character, integrity, and the value of hard work. I was particularly fortunate to have my natural father and my stepfather. Both played different, but huge roles in my life and in my career. My mother made enormous sacrifices for me, and she, on several occasions, was particularly adept at lifting me up in my childhood when I needed it most. Her belief in my abilities were critical to my success in all aspects of life.

None of my success would have been possible without the love, support, and tireless work of my wife, Cindy, of 44 years who did so much for our household and family while I was preoccupied with my work. She additionally provided many valuable comments and corrections on several drafts of the manuscripts that have substantially improved the final product. My two wonderful kids, of whom I am so proud, and my grandchildren inspire me every day to be the best I can be.

To all of you, my success truly has been your success. Thank you.

About the Author

Gary Garfield is a lawyer by training. He practiced law, mostly civil litigation, for several years, representing some of the largest and most respected companies in the country. He joined Bridgestone Americas in its law department, and was the General Counsel and Chief compliance Officer before he was promoted to CEO. Garfield ultimately became its CEO, president, and chairman of the board. He also was an executive vice president of Bridgestone Corporation and a member of its Global Executive Committee. Currently, Garfield is a writer, keynote speaker, consultant, and executive coach. He is very proud to have been a guest lecturer at numerous institutions, including Yale University, West Point, Vanderbilt University, and The Ohio State University. He also has been an opinion editor contributor for several publications. Gary is involved in raising awareness to our climate crisis, enjoys golf, reading, and, most of all, playing with his grandkids.

Index